Blogging for Profits

ASTRID NICHOLLS

Already Available in the Business Focus Series:

AdSense Publishing

Coming Soon:

Start in ePublishing
Start Your Own Record Label

Visit Fresh Publishing at www.freshpublishing-house.co.uk

Blogging for Profits

ASTRID NICHOLLS

Fresh Publishing
Books... A better way!

First published in Great Britain in 2012
by Fresh Publishing
Skype: fresh.publishing
Website: www.freshpublishing-house.co.uk

ISBN (pbk): 978-1-46993-456-3
ISBN (ebk): 978-1-4658-5439-1

NOTE: The material set out in this book is only for general guidance. Laws and regulations are complex and constantly changing. Readers should check the current position with the relevant authorities before making personal and/or business arrangements. The author and the publisher cannot accept any liability for loss or expenses incurred as a result of relying on any statement made in the book in particular circumstances.

Image Credits

Cover image: digitalart / FreeDigitalPhotos.net

Small chapter images:
Post-it blog: jaylopez / sxc.hu
Relaxed blog icon: LuMaxArt under Creative Common Attribution-ShareAlike 2.0 Generic

Main parts images:
Introduction: Jonny Goldstein under Creative Common Attribution 2.0 Generic
Research and Development: Jonny Goldstein under Creative Common Attribution 2.0 Generic
Starting Up: renjith krishnan / FreeDigitalPhotos.net
Expanding: Idea go / FreeDigitalPhotos.net

Creative Common Licences can be found at the following web addresses:
Creative Common Attribution-ShareAlike 2.0 Generic
→ http://creativecommons.org/licenses/by-sa/2.0/deed.en

Attribution 2.0 Generic
→ http://creativecommons.org/licenses/by/2.0/

Contents

1 – Introduction

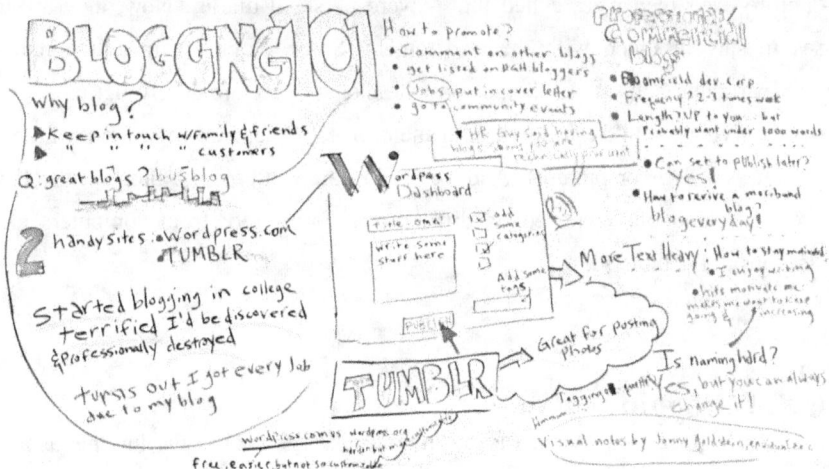

1.1 Introduction to Blogging

Nowadays a blog can be many things, and serve a wide variety of purposes. The very first blogs – before even they were called that – were personal diaries. Now, they are used by businesses to stay in touch with their customers. Some blogs are informational, usually focusing on particular subjects or themes – niche blogs. Some are purely fictional – tools for fiction writers trying to build a following for themselves. Others are collections of a particular media – such as videos or pictures. And yet others are multimedia: blogs with all kind of different content, and often viewed on different platforms too; from computers to mobile phones, laptops to PC tablets...

History of Blogging

Blogging did not appear as suddenly as you may think. The idea of the Internet as a mean of expressing your ideas and communicating with others has always been around. Websites always were an excellent way of showing others what you are interested in, or in the case of a business, what you have to offer. And email soon became a favourite mean of communication: after all, it's free, instantaneous, and international.

People on the Internet very quickly grabbed onto the fact that the Web could allow them to make themselves heard. Even the basic web page was a way to spread your message. In the

2

Blog

mid 90's, many people were using simple web pages and websites as personal diaries. It was a past-time best reserved to those with at least some basic HTML or coding. With only little help available in the form of web designing software, it was best you already knew what you were doing. In particular if you wanted your site to look half way decent. But just like in real life, what people really wanted to do was communicate. They wanted to both be able to read what someone thought and answer them to present their own views and ideas. This is how online communities and a little later forums started. And software evolved to allow people to write answers to previous entries – thus creating the forum threads.

The blogging revolution started with the arrival of the first dedicated blogging platforms. The very first of them was Open Diary. The site launched in October 1998 and was the first example of the now widely used hosted blog service. In less than 12 months, several other services were launched: LiveJournal started in March 1999, Blogger.com in August and Diaryland in September. With these arrivals, weblogs became accessible to all. Knowledge of HTML, although useful, was no longer necessary to keep a site.

It is also in early 1999 that the term blog first appeared. It first started as a joke when Peter Merholz transformed weblog into we blog on his own site. The term caught the eye of Evan Williams, co-founder of Pyra Labs and one of the brains behind Blogger.com. This is where the name of the platform comes from. It soon led the term to become widely used – both as a noun and a verb.

Blogging as a Business

One thing that cannot be stressed enough is that you should not launch into any kind of business without researching carefully. Sadly, too many people think that starting their own business is something easy enough. They then run into trouble when they realize they have no idea on how to find and secure orders. Let's try and avoid this mistake here and learn as much as we can about blogging before we launch.

The Blogging Industry

It is actually not that simple to learn anything about the statistics of blogging for profit. This is because although it is now recognized as an online industry, blogging is still mostly viewed as a tool by the business community rather than a business opportunity. The shift has only recently started and data can be hard to come by.

In 2005, Technorati reported to be tracking 14.2 million blogs. By June 2008, they had indexed over 112.8 millions blogs since their 2002 debuts. By the end of 2009, the number was 133 million and still growing. This is a pretty impressive growth of just over 835% over 4 years. True these numbers may also include abandoned and spam blogs. But this just illustrates how popular the medium is and how much it is being used.

If you are looking for data about blogging, and how much it holds over consumers, read the State of the Blogosphere reports that Technorati publishes every year. According to State of the Blogosphere 2011, 18% of bloggers did so as a way to create an income – either to supplement their primary income, or to replace it altogether. 8% are asked to blog as part of their current job. And 13% are entrepreneurs, blogging as part of their own business operations. You are looking to join one – or more – of these segments. Technorati have also found that consumers now trust bloggers more than they do mainstream media. These numbers speak for themselves: blogging is becoming a lucrative business model for many. And competition is hotting up very quickly.

Tip:
Although information on the blogging industry is a bit scarce, it does exist. Go to your local business agency or Chamber of Commerce, and see if they can help with your research.

When it comes to sub-markets – or niches, as bloggers call them – blogging works similarly to its parent industry, publishing. First, markets are separated by broad age groups – adults and children. Then they are separated by subjects. Unlike traditional publishing however, blogging niches can be extremely narrow. Where publishers have to target broad demographics in order to recoup their investments, bloggers can cater to very small markets because of the low overheads of running a blog. So if a publisher produces a book on how to train your dog, as a blogger you can target people looking to teach their dogs to dance.

The Blogging Model

As you enter the blogging market, you will effectively become a publisher. A provider of information. Readers will come to you for one or more of these reasons:

- they want to know more about your chosen subject;

- they want to learn the latest news about that subject;

- they want to know your opinion about an issue;

- they are researching a product or service relating to your subject.

As a blogger, you will be offering this and maybe even more. However, you are at a disadvantage compared to traditional publishers. Books, magazines and newspapers mostly have models where the readers pays for the information. Blogging is traditionally a free medium. And so, in order to make your business viable, you need a clearly defined strategy to bring money in.

Typically, there are three ways to make money using a blog:

- advertising;

- affiliate marketing, and;

- selling products.

We will take a closer look at these and other income generation methods in a later chapter.

Blogging – Where to Start?

Tip:

Grab pen and paper now. Keep notes as you read through this book and jot down ideas and questions as they occur to you. There is too much to remember and do when starting a business. Don't rely solely on your memory.

If you are entirely new to the world of blogging, the first thing you should do is read from the blogosphere. Just go to Google Blog Search, Blogger.com, WordPress.com, Technorati, LiveJournal... and search for blogs to read. See what is out there and get a feel of what you'd like to do with your blog. You don't have to worry about choosing a theme or subject yet. You don't even need to worry about how you will make money. The aim of this exercise is simply to see what others are doing, and get a vague idea of how you will do things on your own blog.

Once you have a good idea of what your favourite style(s) are, you can decide on your platform. There are many software for you to choose from in order to create a blog. In effect, blogging software are specialized Content Management Systems or CMS allowing the author/editor/manager of a blog to easily create and edit posts and manage comments left by readers. Other useful features can be added to the core software to customize it further to your particular needs.

There are far too many possible software and services to use in order to create a blog for us to list here. So here are some of the most used:

- ⏱ WordPress – This is one of the major players in blogging today. It is easy to use, and is quite powerful thanks to the numerous plugins maintained by the community. What's more, it's open source, and so the actual core software is free. With WordPress, you also have the choice between the hosted and self-hosted versions.

- ⏱ Blogger – Just like WordPress, it is free. It also has the clout of Google behind it. Blogger is a hosted software, meaning that as soon as you register, you will be able to blog. No need to go through installing the software anywhere.

- ⏱ TypePad – This one is widely used by some of the major broadcasting corporations – such as the BBC, CBC and Sky News to maintain their blogs. You will have to pay a monthly fee to access the software, but hosting is included.

- ⏱ Movable Type – If you decide on using this software for your business, keep in mind you will need to purchase a license for the Pro version.

- ⏱ Drupal – This is a more general CMS than the more specialized ones cited above, but it is widely used to create blogs anyway. This is only for those willing to self host their site.

Laws and Regulations

This is an area that many people choose to ignore, thinking they now very well what can and cannot be done. We suggest that you at least read through it. You will be surprised at the amount of things you may learn.

> **Warning:**
>
> This is only an overview of the laws you may fall under. Keep in mind that more rules and regulations may be passed at any time. Also remember that rules differ between countries, and you should be aware that what is legal in one country is not necessarily so in another.

Copyright Laws

Copyright is something that will both protect you and something you have to follow. In the UK, anything you create is copyrighted automatically to you. There's no need to register anything so long as you can prove you wrote it. You should note that it is only the actual written words that are copyrighted: ideas are not, and nothing stops a competitor from taking your idea, putting their own spin on it and publishing their own work. They just can't use your words or create a work that is too obviously taken from your own. Copyright for written work last 70 years from the death of the author.

Copyright is also something you will need to careful respect as a professional blogger. Just as you do not want people using your work without permission, most other works are protected. On the Internet, everything is copyrighted, even if people tend to forget that since it can be accessed for free.

In order to use materials – that could be posts from other bloggers, pictures, videos or other media – you have found on the Internet, or even offline, you must first find out who holds the copyright and what kind of rights are available to the work. For example, most books and ebooks are usually 'all rights reserved'. This means you cannot use the material within in any way without the permission of either the publishers or the authors, depending on who holds the rights you are looking to exploit. The best way to find out what right are available is to track down the copyright holder.

The Internet has also encouraged the rise of three license types that could be advantageous to you. PLR is an abbreviation for Private Label Right. The most usual definition for this license is that you can reuse the PLR work and claim it as your own without even editing it. One should be careful to read the license properly as not all PLR license gives away all rights.

The second license type to look out for is CC, or Creative Commons. CC actually host a wide variety of licenses. Creative Commons is a non-profit organization based in the US. Their licenses were created to help share creative works in a legal manner. So long as the license allows the work to be used for commercial purposes, you can use it.

Finally Public Domain defines all the works with expired copyrights. As mentioned above, written works stay copyrighted for 70 years after the death of the author in the UK. Musical compositions are copyrighted for 70 years as well. The actual recordings of these compositions are copyright for 50 years after their first release.

Ecommerce Regulations

The Internet is a non-place to which each country around the world is trying to apply their own set of laws. Your customers could come from any part of the world and have very different laws when it come to doing business online. These regulations make it a requirement to tell your customers that they are agreeing to the laws of your country – or at least the laws of the country your business is based.

You need to give your customers a certain number of information about your business. Your business name, address, and other contact details – such as website, email address, phone and fax numbers... should be shown. You should also have things like your VAT registration number – if any – and details of the professional bodies you are a member of. If you have to report to a particular body for regulation purposes, you should also have their details

Laws and Regulations

somewhere on your site. These do not have to appear on every pages of your site. Most people simply put these details in their 'About Us' page, and/or in their Terms and Conditions.

If you display your prices on your site, you must indicate whether or not they include taxes and delivery costs. You should explain clearly how to fill the order form and offer your customer a way to go back and correct errors. Also you have to give your customers the opportunity to print a copy of their order for their own records. This can be either by presenting them with a page to print with a summary of their order, or by sending them an email with all the relevant details.

The Distance Selling Regulations 2000

These regulations aim to protect consumers who are not present when buying something. This is why they would apply to you. Technically, they would only apply if you sell your own products, but it is always good to check that your affiliate partners are following most of these rules. If they do not and your readers get in trouble on that site, it could harm your relationship with them.

According to this set of rules, you should have on your site, or offer during the ordering process, the following details:

- details of the supplier;

- terms and conditions, including how to cancel and complain, any guarantees, and customer services after the sale;

- confirmation of the order;

- delivery times.

Consumers are also allowed to change their mind within 7 days, starting from the day they receive what they have ordered. If you forget to write down about this in your terms and conditions, the cooling off period is automatically extended to 3 months.

Data Protection Act 1998

The Data Protection Act deals with the information you request from your customers. You can only ask for the information you truly need for delivering your products or services. If you keep a database of past customers, you must keep it up to date, and allow the people on it to access and change the data as and when they wish to do so. You obviously also have to keep these details secure, and should not give them away or pass them on to third parties unless your customer has agreed to it or it is necessary for you to do business. If you have to transfer the data to a country outside of the European Economic Area, you must make sure the data will be stored securely in that other country as well.

Libel

There is a famous phrase in the world of publishing: 'Publish and be damned.' As soon as you hit the publish button on your blog, you will become entirely responsible for what the post says about people. And this mean you could be sued for libel: the publication of false statements with the intent to harm a person's good name and reputation.

This is where you have to make sure that everything you write is actually true. If you are reporting on rumours, you should check carefully whether this could be true and word your post carefully. Even the use of words like rumour, alleged, and supposed, will not stop people from suing you if they think they have a case.

Checklist

To Do:

- ✔ Read blogs.

- ✔ Read some more blogs.

- ✔ Keep track of every ideas and questions that occurs to you.

- ✔ Research the laws involved carefully, to be sure you understand what you let yourself into.

1.2 Is this right for you?

You now have a better idea of what may be involved in owning your own blogging business. The questions you have to ask yourself now is: can you actually work for yourself? And if you can, is blogging the right business for you?

The Entrepreneur Mindset

Before you actually go any further, you should really sit down and work out if you are cut out to be an entrepreneur. If we were to ask, you would probably tell us that you are attracted to the lifestyle: being your own boss, working your own hours, the potential of earning millions as your business takes off, more times to spend with your family and enjoying life...

The problem is that this view of the self-employed life is for those who have been in business for years and have managed to make a real success of their business. Starting up is a lot of hard work. It will take you a lot of time. To start a successful business, you will need a set of skills – both personal and business-related. Some of them can be taught. Others are more difficult to acquire if you don't have them already.

Blog

The Entrepreneur Mindset

Your **personal skills** should include:

- motivation;

- organization;

- multi-tasking;

- evaluating situations, and;

- making decisions.

Those are the skills difficult to acquire if you do not naturally own them. That does not mean you cannot train yourself to become all of those things.

Motivation is probably the best tool in your arsenal when starting your own business. Here is a painful statistic for you: it takes an average of 3 years to establish a business, and most fail within the first 12 to 18 months. You will need to stay motivated through these difficult few months. There are many reasons to start a business. Surprisingly, making money is not usually high on the list.

Most people hope for a better lifestyle – a better family-work balance. Others just want to be their own boss and have no one to answer to. Some have simply always dreamed of starting their own business. In our current economy, people who have been made redundant and those who can't find full-time jobs take this step as a way to get back to work and earn a living. Just find your motivation and keep it in mind through the rough times.

People tend to start a blogging business because it is easy enough. As most online businesses, it can established from home without any trouble. It also allows to start part-time if necessary, working around your primary job.

Organizational skills are needed by anyone in business. There are a lot of things you need to keep track in a business: work deadlines, stocks, sales, payments dues and received, customers problems, taxes... And if you forget some of them, you could very well get in trouble. Some people are naturally more organized than others. But anyone can learn to work more efficiently. Make good use of the features most phones now boost: calendars, alarms, and memos can help you remember everything you need to do.

Blogging adds to this the needs to research your subjects, write and edit your posts, and keep up with the news in your chosen subject(s). As your business grow, you may also need to find freelancers, and keep track of the work they do for you, its quality, and the payments you make to them.

Multi-tasking is an off-shoot of your organizational skills that will need to be developed fairly quickly. Most of the time you will be working on different jobs at the same time. And you will probably need to accomplish all of them to strict deadlines. Blogging in itself is simple enough. The problems really start when you have two or more sites to update every day or so. If you want to create enough posts to update your site(s) regularly, you will need to research several articles at the same time. You will also need to market your business and your sites continuously in order to keep bringing traffic in. If you are building a list alongside your site, you will also need to create and sent your newsletter regularly to keep the attention of your readers.

The last two skills we have listed previously – evaluating situations and making decisions – are probably the most important skills for you to develop. Everyone uses these skills in everyday life. You find that your favourite shoes have a split across the sole. You need to buy a new pair, so you check how much you can afford to spend. You look for a new pair of shoes and find several you like. Finally you decide on the best pair according size, style, colour, and price.

This example may be simplistic, but you established what your problem was, its solution, then worked your way to that solution. You need to apply those same skills in your everyday business life. You must be able to see the threats to, and opportunities for, your business before your competition. You should then plan how best to overcome difficulties and take advantage of circumstances as they occur. This is where market research really comes in handy, as it can help you to identify threats and opportunities before they affect your business too much.

14

Personal skills as good habits

Do not despair if you find that you possess only one or two of these personal skills. Look at it this way: personal skills are only good habits to be taken and consistently applied to your life. To be organized, you only need to make use of all the tools available to keep your work load compartmentalized. Calendars, diaries, memos, reminders on your phone, project management software... All of this can be used to help you.

If you find your motivation fails you from time to time, keep yourself motivated. Write down exactly why you are starting your blogging business and display this prominently on your work space. Look at this list when you feel down and remind yourself why you're working so hard.

When it comes to evaluation and decision-making, your best bet is to look at what other entrepreneurs are doing. Look for news from the past few years and see how different businesses reacted to the same piece of news in their industry. Work out what you would have done and if it would have been successful. Talk to other local entrepreneurs and see what they are doing in response to their own threats and problems. Help them if you can, and they might help you in return.

Business Skills

All of these can be learned at your local college, at home with the help of books or through the Internet. Following are the very basic skills you should acquire if you don't already have them:

- an understanding of selling;

- negotiation skills;

- customer service skills, and;

- book-keeping.

The best way to learn about selling is to get a job in sales. It is unlikely – although not impossible – that your local college will have a course focusing on selling. A broader business course will probably teach you the basics, if you are willing to spend longer on studying. Alternatively, you could try to pick the brains of a few friends and acquaintances working in sales. Learning from books is also an option. Whatever your way of learning, remember to monitor your results. This will help you to establish the best techniques for your business.

What you need to remember is that you rarely get a second chance to sell with blogging. If you don't grab your readers attention from the start, they are likely to go off and never come back. And if you do manage to transform them into recurring readers – or even better, subscribers – they will only read your posts once. You need to make sure that every single of your selling tools – whether they are reviews, banner ads, or even the design of your site – are optimized to ensure sales.

The one good thing is that your readers will be somewhat interested in what you're selling, so long as it is relevant to your subject. There remains the problem of directing interested people to your blog, but we will discussed this in more details later. Having interested people on your site, you simply need to convince them that a particular product may be the solution to their problem.

In the world of blogging, **negotiation skills** are probably not used as much as in some other businesses. Most of online transaction do not allow for bartering. This is particularly true as you are starting your online venture. However, as your blogging business grows, you may find you need to negotiate contracts with freelancers. If you grow large enough, and know your suppliers face-to-face, you may also want to negotiate with them to get better discounts, commissions, and/or prices for the services they provide you.

As with selling skills, **customer service skills** are better experienced than taught. There is nothing better to prepare you to deal with a difficult customer than facing one. Dealing with customers through your blog will be quite different than having one on the phone. Most complaints will come in the forms of comments or emails.

Never reply to a bad comment or email in anger. People are entitled to their opinions and more often than not it will be very different from what you think. Even if the comment is really rude, take a day or so to think up a polite reply explaining your point of view, or describing the useful features of a particular product.

Business Skills

Book-keeping is one business skill you really should invest in. It is a legal requirement for you to keep records of every transactions made by your business. This is also important to work out your accounts. Some people prefer not to get involved in this and leave it all to their accountant. Others will pay for a book-keeper to go through the trouble of putting all the records in shape, ready for the accountant to prepare the accounts.

I believe book-keeping is too important a job to leave it to another, in particular at the beginning of your business. Through book-keeping, you will always know how much your business is spending on what and when. You will also know how much money you have in your account and whether or not you can afford that marketing campaign you are thinking about.

Blogging Skills

Blogging does not require much more than the skills we have discussed previously. For the sake of completeness, here are the skills that are particular to blogging:

- an understanding of computer technologies;

- researching;

- writing, and;

- editing.

As we have already noted, blogging has been made very easy with the arrival of dedicated software. However, you still need to know the basics behind using a computer, and web hosting. You will need to learn to use your chosen blogging software, and how to design your site around it. Without this basic understanding, starting a blogging business could be a lot harder for you. If you are not already familiar with computers, a course at your local college is probably the best thing for you.

When it comes to web hosting, the best place to start is the Internet. There are plenty of places offering free hosting. This will allow you to familiarize yourself with what will be require to work your business. Byet Host is a decent company offering free hosting. Their free account may not be suitable for your business, but it's a good place to learn about web hosting.

We have already had a look at several software to power your blog. Once you have chosen yours, set a training blog up for yourself. This will allow you to work out exactly how the system works and if it is really for you. Most blogging software have a community of users willing to help new comers who run into trouble. Once you have chosen you blogging platform, you can learn to design around the software. Or look for ready-made themes fitting your subject.

Researching is important. After all, you will not know everything about your subject and will at least need to stay up to date with the latest developments and news in your chosen subject. However, research should not stop at what news story or review to write next.

You should always keep an eye on your readers as well. See where they come from, if they subscribe to your blog and how. If you can, find out about their demographics – age, gender, where they're from, education level, marital status... All of this will allow you to tailor both your writing and your marketing efforts to reach as many people fitting this profile as possible.

Obviously **writing** is a very important skill for a blogging entrepreneur. You need to develop your own peculiar style. This will be an additional hook, that will hopefully get your readers to come back regularly to read your newest posts. The better you write and the more unique your style, the greater the chances to transform occasional readers into subscribers.

Remember that you will also need to sell products and services through your blog posts. In order to do so successfully, you need to convince your readers that buying whatever it is you are promoting is a good idea. With that in mind, it might also be a good idea to invest in a book to teach you the basic of copywriting – the art of writing advertising and promotional copy.

Editing is also a good skill – or rather set of skills – to have. Of course, most of us now use word processors with built-in spellcheckers. And many blogging platforms have also a spell-checking feature included. However, these generally don't account for grammar: they don't make a difference between its and it's, there and their... It's all good to a spellchecker so long as the word is in their database.

It's true that writing style is generally informal on blogs. But bad grammar, and glaring mistakes will turn off even the most relaxed readers. Always take the time to proofread your post after letting it lie for an hour or two. It can only improve your writing.

Experience or Not?

Actually, this is the one thing you do not need to start a blogging business. So long as you have a good grasp of writing, and are eager to learn everything you can about your chosen subject, you can blog. There are no course for you to take in order to fulfil a legal requirement. All you really need is good writing and good ideas for posts.

There are plenty of people online who have started with no previous business experience. They learned on the job, so to speak. You can do exactly the same thing. There's little doubt you will make mistakes, but so have others before you. It's just how you will learn.

Obviously, any kind of experience will allow you to start better and quicker. Any professional writing experience will give you confidence for researching, writing and editing your posts. Any customer service experience will help you to handle your readers and harsh critics.

And if you want that experience, you can still go and get it. Go to your local newspaper and see if they would allow you in their office to see how things work. Talk with journalists and see if they can give you some tips. Go to your local charity shop and volunteer for a few hours. This will give you some hands on experience of dealing with customers. Ask your local Business Link office or Chamber of Commerce if there are seminars or events you could attend in your area. Contact other blogging entrepreneurs and ask for their advice. Although busy, most will recognize themselves in you and might be willing to help.

The Money Problem

This is probably the one thing that stop most people from starting a business. It can be very expensive. Blogging is probably one of the cheapest way to set up a business. But it will still require a good amount of money from you before you start breaking even – not even mentioning making a profit.

No business can start without a solid amount of money in the bank to deal with all the costs associated with starting and running a business. After all you will need a computer, access to the Internet, a printer for the paperwork, a desk to put it all on, a locking filing cabinet to keep all your records safely in, and a small budget for marketing purposes. And that's before you look into stock, product creation, promotional items, accountant fees, training costs...

You need to keep in mind that for the few months at least – maybe for as long as the first 3 years – you will not earn enough to live off your earning. All the money will have to be ploughed back into your business. Even when you finally reach the break-even point, most of your profits will have to be put back into the business in order to make it grow. All this means that you will not be able to make a living from your business. As such, you need to make sure you either have enough savings to live off, or have access to another source of income.

Checklist

To Do:

✓ Evaluate your personal skills. Can you cut it in the business world, or should you re-think your decision to start working for yourself?

✓ Take a serious look at your current business and blogging skills and evaluate where you fail to meet the basic requirements.

✓ Find training opportunities. How much it would cost you to brush up your skills, or learn new one?

2 – Research and Development

2.1 Business Basics

Now that you know a bit more about blogging in general, let's see what it takes to start a business. There are a few things you need to know and some decisions for you to make.

Legal Structure

There are four basic business structures to choose from in the UK:

- Sole trader

- Partnership

- Limited company

- Limited liability partnership

Most bloggers remain sole traders – or the foreign equivalent – quite simply because it is the easiest way to set up and run a business. You only need to let HM Revenue & Customs (HMRC) know that you have started your own business so they can update their records and send you your Tax Return and your National Insurance contribution bills.

24

Blog

Legal Structure

Trading this way, you retain total control and ownership of your business. You also have to accept all the risks, and you will be personally liable for your business's debts. The one good point is that you get to keep all the profits.

A partnership works in more or less the same way as being a sole trader, except you will have – and be – a partner. If you have a friend or a member of your family who knows what they're talking about, know their way around a blog and the Internet, or at least are willing to learn, you can set up together. You will share the work-load, the responsibilities and the profits.

If you decide to go down this way, it is preferable to draw up a contract detailing who has invested how much, who is supposed to do what in the business, and how the profits will be split between the partners. The partnership will need to be registered with HMRC by a designated partner. This partner will then be responsible for filing the Self Assessment Partnership Tax Return, on behalf of the partnership. Each of the partners will need to contact the HMRC to declare their own share of the profits through the Self Assessment tax return. Each will also all need to their own National Insurance contributions.

A word of advice: avoid splitting the business in equal shares as it can lead to serious arguments and problems when one partner decides it's time to leave. The person doing the majority of the work should have a bigger share of the business.

Limited companies – or Ltd – involve a lot more paperwork to create and to run than the other two alternatives. It also involves many fees – some of them recurring each year. You will need to register with Companies House, either by filling the registration form yourself, by asking a formation agent or using Business Link's web incorporation service. You will also have to file your accounts each year – and pay another fee for this. As well as sending paperwork to Companies House, you need to keep quite a bit around your office.

There are two big advantages to setting up a limited company. The first is that it is completely independent to you financially. If the company gets in debt, it will not mean you will. And if the business fails, you will only lose the money you have actually put into it. The second is it might be easier to secure funding. In any case, you would then have a chance to access venture funding or business angels.

Limited Liability Partnerships – or LLP – fall right between a Ltd and a partnership. Like a company, you need to register with Companies House, appoint an auditor if needed, and if the business fails you would only loose the money you put in the partnership. You will have to send a set of accounts and an annual return to Companies House each year and tell them when changes occur in the partnership.

However a LLP works like a normal partnership when it comes to taxes. One member will be named responsible for the Self Assessment Partnership tax return, and each member will also have to file a Self Assessment for their own share of the profit and pay for NIC.

Your Business Name

Many people who start a business simply trade under their own name. However, it might be just as easy to name your business after your first blog. If you are already planning a blogging empire, you may want to choose something that will relate to blogging, publishing, or your chosen niche if you are not planning to depart from it.

Brainstorm a few names. You can even rope in a few friends to give you a hand if you want. Have a look at what other blogs in your niche call themselves. Be careful not to choose a name too similar as you could lose traffic to them if people simply type your business name in their search engine. Watch out for trademarks. These are names other businesses have claimed for their own. You cannot use them.

A good way to look for business names and trademarks that have already been registered is to go on the National Business Register website. They keep a database of current trademarks, limited companies names and domain names in use, and also manage a database for registered sole traders and partnerships names. Alternatively, you can contact Companies House to see what names limited companies currently trading have chosen.

Premises

As a professional blogger, you will probably be working from home. This can have advantages. You get to save on petrol and lease costs. You might even be able to claim some tax-relief for using your home as your office. But it can be difficult to make the difference between work and family life. The best way to achieve this to set yourself strict business hours, and stick to them. Make sure that your family and friends know about this too and respect your working hours. Of course, you will be able to be flexible when it comes to working hours and breaks. But it is important that your life does not encroach too much on your business, and same the other way around.

When it comes to your workspace, you may not need much. A decent workstation, with a couple of filing cabinets or cupboards to keep your paperwork safely locked away, might be enough. Because you will be spending a lot of time seating at your computer screen, you may want to invest in a very good office chair and wrist rest for your keyboard. This might minimize the risks of back and wrist troubles associated with typing all day. You should also make sure you sit far enough from the screen to reduce eye strain and headaches. This is actually quite important, in particular if you work alone. Repetitive strain injury, back strains and severe headaches could all stop you from working. Which in turns would mean a loss of a revenue for your business.

If you have enough capital and are looking to create a partnership or employ staff, you may want to look into renting an office from the beginning. You probably can find some office space near you. Remember to read through the lease carefully to find out exactly what it is you are taking on. Alternatively, you could look into teleworking. This has been made a lot easier by advances in the Internet and software. Investing in a good ERP or CRM software to create an Intranet alongside your main website/blog, along with Skype and email to handle communications, and any of your employees could easily work from home - just like you!

Records and Book-keeping

It is a legal requirement to keep track of every transactions your business makes. To do this, you must keep all invoices and receipts you are given for your business. You must also keep a copy of all invoices and receipts you are giving your customers. These will be the proof that you have spent and earned what you declare to the HMRC. You also will need them to work out your accounts.

As I mentioned before, small business owners really should take care of their book-keeping themselves, so that they know precisely how much money comes in and out of their business, and how much they have in reserve. When it comes to your blogging operations, it will probably be more important that you know how much money is coming in rather than out. Your overheads may well only include your Internet connection, web hosting and insurances. But you need to keep a good eye on how much you are earning. This is particularly true if you use several different affiliate programs and advertising networks, as your money will be spread all over the Internet.

Here are a few tips to help you get started:

🕐   Keep all the paper trail.

Each time you spend or receive money on behalf of your business, you should receive or produce a receipt, purchase invoice, sales invoice, commission statement, or some other proof of the transaction. You should keep every single of these to prove that you have paid or receive that money. Other things to keep are bank statements, cheque book stubs, paying in books, copies of your employees' wages slips, Income Tax bill, National Insurance statements, and copies of your VAT statements.

🕐   Keep organized.

It will save you a lot of headaches if you stay on top of your book-keeping. Dedicate an hour each week to deal with the paperwork. Work out the more efficient filing system for you – whether this is keeping everything ordered by date or another way. The quicker you find what you need from your records, the less time you will have to spend on this. Keep additional notes to remind you exactly what you bought or why you were paid. There's another important reason to keep things organized: the quicker your accountant can find his way around your books, the less money you will have to pay them.

🕐   Accounting books or software

Records and Book-keeping

This can be an important choice for anyone in business. Do you want an easy accounting system in the form of a book to be filled in weekly or monthly, or do you want to spend some time learning to use an accounting software that will be more powerful and offer more options?

Books like the Simplex D system by Simplex or The Best Small Business Accounts Book by Hingston Publishing are useful as they allow you to easily work out your accounts.

Software such as Sage and Quickbooks are the favourite amongst accountants. Use them if you're going to outsource your final accounts to your local accountant. If you are going to work out your accounts yourself, you may want to try GnuCash or AdminSoft. Both take a bit of getting used to, but they have the advantage of being free and automatically producing many financial reports for your business, including your Profit & Loss report.

Taxes

Sole traders and partners are liable for both Class 2 and Class 4 National Insurance contributions. Class 2 NIC are a flat fee tax, currently £2.50 per week. Class 4 is paid based on your profits declared on your Tax return. You can be exempt of both if your earn below a certain limit – currently £5,315 for Class 2 and £7,225 for Class 4. You have to ask to be exempt from Class 2 NIC and fill a form. As a professional blogger, it is unlikely you will earn this much in your first year, so you might as well get hold of this form and fill it in immediately. Each tax year, you should receive your Tax return and Self Assessment forms. These must be in by the 31 October if you use paper returns and by 31 January if doing your returns online.

If you decide to set up a limited company, as a company director you will have to pay Class 1 NIC unless your earning for the current tax years are less than £7,225. You will also be responsible for working out how much corporation tax you owe HMRC and for paying this on time. Currently, the rate is 25%. The deadline to pay is 9 months and one day after the end of your accounting period.

VAT stands for value added tax. You should register for VAT if your sales reach £73,000 for the last 12 months. You may also register voluntarily, if it is to your tax advantage. There are three rates of VAT: standard (20%), reduced (5%), and zero-rated (0%). It is up to you to find out what rate applies to your products and to charge that rate to your customers. For example, books are zero-rated, while ebooks are standard-rated goods. You will be charged VAT when buying supplies for your business. If the difference between the amount of VAT you charge your customers (the output tax) is greater than the amount you pay to suppliers (the input tax), you must pay that amount to HMRC. If your input tax is greater than your output tax, HMRC will owe you that difference. Some businesses are eligible to use special schemes to make calculating this difference easier. Your VAT return must be filed and paid within a month of the end of your accounting period. You get a seven-day additional period if you elect to pay electronically.

Employing Staff

It is unlikely you will employ staff as you launch your blogging empire. Most blogs start their lives as one-person businesses. Many never grow to become more. As you think about launching your business, you need to decide if you can commit the numerous hours needed to launch your blog, or if you need someone to take some of the strain in exchange for a greater financial investment on your part.

There is a lot of paperwork involved in employing staff. For first timers, it can look like a real minefield. You will take on many new responsibilities and failing to meet the laws and regulations involved can be costly. Some of these include:

- National Minimum Wage

- Collecting tax from your employees

- Statutory sick and maternity pay

The first thing you should to is contact HMRC and get your hands on a New Employer Starter Pack. This will answer many of your questions, and should help you get ready to recruit. If you have more questions, have a look on the Business Link website. They have lots of information available.

Insurances

You could be forgiven to think that a blogging business has very little to think about when it comes to insurance. In actual fact, this is something you should think very carefully about. A great many things can go wrong. You should be certain you have some kind of contingency plan in place if the worst does happen. There are four insurances every bloggers should think about as they are very relevant.

The first is **professional indemnity cover**, if people decide to sue you because they feel you have given them bad advice. Sadly, this happens more and more often. Even if you can prove you did things perfectly right, you will have to deal with upfront legal expenses. Professional Indemnity will cover these and any damages awarded by the courts.

Copyright insurance covers you for in two particular cases:

- where someone has stolen your copyrighted work;

- where you inadvertently used copyrighted material.

The insurance will usually pay for your legal expenses and cover any damages that may be awarded to the other party.

Libel insurance is also important to bloggers. As a publisher, you will be held responsible if you publish something untrue and/or damaging to the reputation of someone else. It is also true that some people will raise a fuss over things that have been said while they are still true. Usually, this insurance covers legal costs and damages awarded.

Business equipment cover is pretty much vital to you as well. As you rely heavily on your computer, you need to know what happens if it breaks or gets stolen. It could set you back by quite a lot both in terms of time and money. Actual covers vary between insurers but you should get at the very least loss, damage (including accidental damage), and theft.

Other insurances are available, depending on exactly what you are doing. Public Liability is required if members of the public – such as your readers or potential clients looking to use your services – come to visit your offices. Employers' Liability is also required if you employ someone. Business Interruption and Income Protection insurances could help you keep going if something happen either to your business or you. Product Liability could be something you want to look into if you are offering a physical product. Legal expenses could help cover costs for court actions that your normal policy doesn't.

Checklist

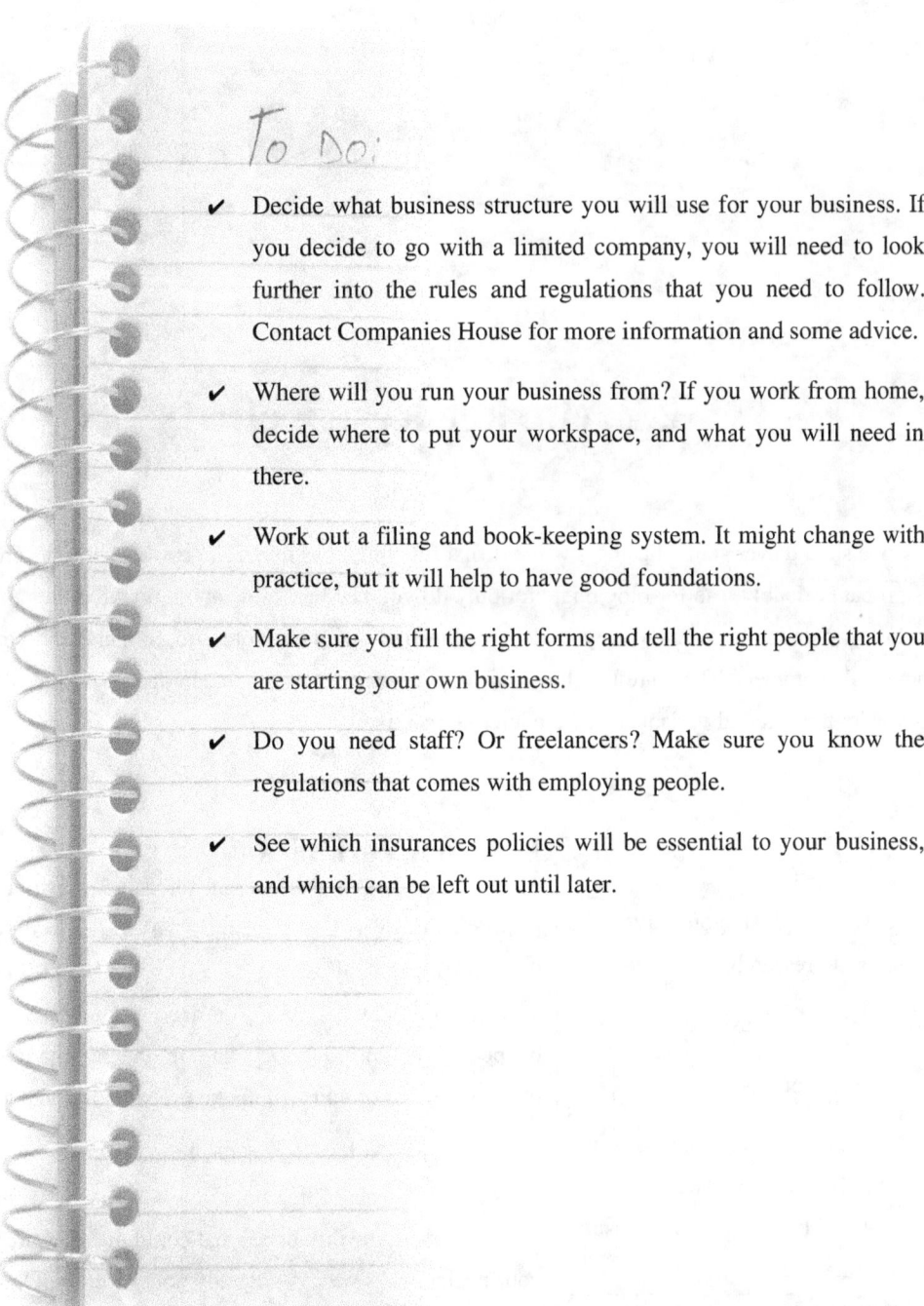

To Do:

✔ Decide what business structure you will use for your business. If you decide to go with a limited company, you will need to look further into the rules and regulations that you need to follow. Contact Companies House for more information and some advice.

✔ Where will you run your business from? If you work from home, decide where to put your workspace, and what you will need in there.

✔ Work out a filing and book-keeping system. It might change with practice, but it will help to have good foundations.

✔ Make sure you fill the right forms and tell the right people that you are starting your own business.

✔ Do you need staff? Or freelancers? Make sure you know the regulations that comes with employing people.

✔ See which insurances policies will be essential to your business, and which can be left out until later.

2.2 Market Research

No one should ever start a business without first finding out as much as possible about it. This is probably doubly true for blogging. Not only do you need to know about how the blogging industry is doing in general, but you also need to find out about your chosen niche and your potential customers. There are two broad areas to research before you can decide if your idea is viable: the external variables, and the internal factors.

Tip:
Remember that you have two things to research:
• your business, and;
• your niche.
You can do both at the same time, since the two will be related, but keep the results separate.

External Variables

This term represents the external forces you have little to no control over. Every business has to be aware of these or risk making wrong decisions that could bring down a blooming business. You need to know what is happening in your industry and in the international business circles or you will not be prepared for change.

We have already introduced the blogging industry in the second chapter of this book. Now we need to find out more about the influences that could make or break your business. As we have already noted, you will have

little power to change any of these facts as the decisions are made by people outside of your influence. But knowing what is coming could allow you to react quicker.

PESTEL Analysis

For those who may not know, PESTEL stands for Political, Economical, Social, Technological, Environmental and Legal analysis. It is important to conduct such work as it allows you to identify threats and opportunities to your business coming from outside the industry. A thorough analysis of these outside influence can also assure your potential investors you are aware how the rest of the world may impact your business.

> **Tip:**
>
> Researching the markets for your niche subject is not all that different from researching the market for your blogging business. You can use the same tools and techniques, only with a different focus.

Although the PESTEL analysis never is the first thing to appear in a marketing plan, it is a good starting point for you to learn more both about the blogging industry and your niche. As a blogger, you should analyse both the blogging industry and that of your chosen subject, in order to gain a greater understanding of the problems your blog might run into, and the problems your blog readers might want to know and learn more about.

Below is a simplified PESTEL analysis of the current situation in the UK for a blogging business, to show what such an analysis could look like. Remember that this analysis may very well be outdated by the time this book is published, so use it as a basis for your own, but do the work!

The UK has seen a **political** change recently with the last election. Corporation tax has gone down again this year and is planned to go down again for the next 3 years. Income tax has been lowered to 20%. This is a good incentive to start a business now, in particular since earning levels have also been raised. The current government is also supposed to try and reduce the red tape associated with running a business in the UK.

Worldwide **economy** has been pretty grim. The recession has hit the UK quite hard. The VAT rates have changed several times over the past few years to respond to the recession. After lowering it to 15% for a year, it went back to 17.5%, then up to 20% at the beginning of 2011.

Although no announcement has been made at the time of writing, business owners should be prepared for further changes, depending on how the economy reacts. Recovery started but is now stalling. Growth is slower than anticipated. Disposable incomes are falling. As such, people are less inclined to spend on non-essential. This might make things difficult for bloggers, as most business models relies on blog readers buying through the site. New business models may have to be look into in order to sustain the business.

Social networking has grown in popularity and is still growing. This is because instead of just reading the news, readers can react and discuss it with all their friends. Distance and costs are no longer concern as most social networking sites are international and free. This is a great occasion to engage customers and find out exactly what they think about you, your business and your products. Social networks also provide ways to increase readerships by promoting directly to their users.

Technology is obviously very important to your blogging business. Software have evolved greatly to make blogging a lot easier and faster than it used to. Some blogging platforms – such as WordPress – are constantly being developed both by their creators and by the community and so you have to keep up with these developments. Developers are creating every months new programs to automate posting and/or marketing on your blog. Some are very good programs, others less so and you have to make sure not to get sucked in by their sales pitches.

Environmental regulations rarely applies to blogging, since you do not produce physical waste. However, consumers are now more conscious about their own impact on the environment and that of the businesses they use. On the Internet, this has led to a growth in web hosting companies offering green hosting. It is also worth it to work out your own environmental policy.

Legislation has seen a few changes recently that will affect your business. As of 1st March, the UK Advertising Standards Authority has placed on Internet marketing the same rules that apply to other kind of direct marketing. Ads must not mislead, offend or harm people. There are also many anti-spam legislation in place across the world. Data protection legislation was put in place to help combat spam, among other things. It is important for you to develop a

External Variables

privacy policy that follow the regulation in place and you stick with it. As a blogging entrepreneur, you may very well be entirely exempt from VAT – so long as you do not sell your own products. It should also be noted that the publishing industry is currently fighting to change the VAT rate on ebooks. Currently, physical books are zero-rated goods, while ebooks are standard-rated. The industry is trying to at least bring ebooks to the reduced-rate segment. At current rates, this would mean that instead of 20%, you would only need to charge 5%. VAT on the ebooks you sell. It is also important to remember that the Internet has no uniform laws. Each website is controlled by the laws of the country from which it operates. So you should carefully read contracts when dealing with foreign suppliers.

Your Competition

It is important to study your competition very closely. You should also remember that you will face two very different sorts of competition:

DIRECT competition is made up of all the other businesses offering the same – or very closely related – products and services to yours. In our context, these are blogs, websites, magazines, and even books related to your subject.

INDIRECT competition are external forces vying up for your potential customer's attention and money – such as buying food, paying the bills, going out with friends, watching TV...

Your direct competitors are very important as they can provide benchmarks for your business in terms of offerings, prices and customer service – among other things.

You should learn as much as possible about your competitors. Try to keep up with the news when they are mentioned. If they are limited companies or limited liability partnerships, go to Companies House and ask to see their annual accounts. This can tell you how well they are doing and how much they are spending on business expenditures such as marketing, stock, or personnel.

Visit their offices, shops, and/or websites and experience their customer service. Learn about their brand, prices, their policies, their Unique Selling Point. Find out how they market their website, how easy it is to use and navigate, if they follow the DDA regulations...

Don't focus solely on the major players. Although they are important, they will not be your main competitors unless you have a huge budget to both start your business and market it.

A Strengths, Weaknesses, Opportunities and Threats analysis will help you to both find out more about your competitors and give you a small understanding of what can go wrong in this industry and how you can react to changes for the best. Identifying your competitors' strengths and weaknesses are part of your threats and opportunities. If they are doing something very right, it could take potential customers away for you. If they do something very wrong, it could be a way for you to steal theirs.

You should also remember that not all your competitors will be online. Do not under-estimate newspapers, magazines, books and TV. All these media are sources of information and most are well established and with large budgets.

Your indirect competition – as mentioned before – is everything else that your customer spends time and/or money on. Your potential customers will buy many things in order to fulfil both their basic needs – such as food, clothing, and shelter for example – and desires (pretty much everything else). You will compete for every penny they earn with every other businesses they interact with. Remember as well that you are trying to get regular readers just as much as you want them to buy something from or through you. Everything that uses up time your readers could spend at your website is competition. Your job here will be to find ways to convince your readers it is a better idea to spend their money with – or through – you rather than buying that new book, reading the newspaper, watching TV, or going for a drink with their friends.

Every ideas that may develop when you think about your indirect competition should be jotted down as they can provide good places to start when developing your marketing campaigns. From these notes you will be able to work out precisely what you will be talking about, what writing style you should use given your target market, and you may also find ideas for your first posts.

Internal Factors

These are the things you can change about your business, because you will be making the decisions in the first place. It is important to collect as much information as possible, to make informed decisions. Otherwise, you could set your business up for failure from the start.

The very first task will be to find your niche and then identify your most typical reader. The rest of the decisions will all stem from this, so you need to get it right. Once you have defined this, you will need to organize your marketing mix. Simply put, this is represented by the seven P's in marketing circles: Product (or Service really), Place, Pricing, Promotion, Process, People, and Physical Evidence.

Target Your Markets

This is one of the most important steps for your business, so you have to get it right. When blogging, identifying your market constitute in two things:

1. Choosing your subject

2. Identifying potential customers

Your Niche

As a digital publisher, it is preferable to specialize yourself a little bit in order to reduce the amount of work involved with launching your business. This is why you should choose only one or two subjects to blog about, and they should preferably be somewhat related.

Tip:

Blogging is particular when it comes to the size of markets. Just because you find out during research that your primary target market is very small doesn't mean it isn't worth entering. Actually some say that it is easier to target small "niche" markets where you can identify a gap. Competitors will usually be smaller and easier to take on since they may not have huge marketing budgets – just like you. They may be more numerous though, and market saturation is an element to take into account. A small niche can make it more likely to succeed if you have a small budget.

You also have an advantage over traditional publishers – that is those dealing in books, newspapers and magazines. They have to offer broad enough publications to appeal to a wide audience in order to make profits. They also have to push these publications to potential customers and upsells are rarely possible. You, as a blogger, can target very small niches. Actually, some think it is best to start with smaller niches – smaller subjects – in order to learn the tricks of the trade. You will pull Internet users to you by offering them content they want to know about for free. Then try to upsell that offering by providing additional products or services.

It is not necessary to know about a niche to write about it: this is where researching skills come in handy. However it will cut down on your initial research time if you decide on a niche you know something about. Before you decide on any niche, you will need to make sure that it will be profitable enough to sustain your blog. The best way to find out if a niche is worth pursuing is to use keywords tools to find out how often this niche is being searched for. Google offers a free keyword tool to do that kind of research. It will show you how many searches are done on Google monthly for your keyword and other related ones. It can also show you the results for Google Insight, showing the trends for these keywords over the past 12 months and where the people searching for these terms come from. Although powerful and very useful, these tools based their results on Google searches only. Good and cheap – if not free – alternatives are WordStream and WordTracker.

Once you have found a profitable niche, you need to make sure you can create or source enough content to make your blog an indispensable resource for your readers. The best way is

Internal Factors

to start by researching the industry related to your subject. You can try to work your way through a PESTEL analysis of your industry, which should give you a clear overview of what is happening. It should also give you a lot of ideas to write or talk about on your blog. If you cannot find enough content to keep your readers coming back regularly, this might not be the best blog to start with. As a start-up, it is preferable to find a niche that will keep money coming in.

You should also research what is selling in this industry. Remember that you will be hoping to find products and/or services to resell, advertise, or promote through affiliate marketing. This is how your business will be making its money.

Your Customers

When blogging, your potential customers can be defined as internet users interested in learning more, hearing news about, and reading reviews relating to your chosen niche. From there, it is easy enough to learn a bit more about what your general reader may 'look' like. The best way to learn about the attitudes and habits of a nation is to ask the government. Most countries organize surveys of their population. Most of the data collected in available in one form of the other. In the UK, the Office for National Statistics puts the results on their website and also publishes the results in printed forms. If you are looking for information about US citizen, FedStats is a good place to start. For Europe, you can access Eurostat. When looking for information on a particular country – such as France or Germany – you may well have to translate the information into English. But it may be worth it if you are looking to target this particular market.

Let us start by learning more about UK Internet users. The best place to stay up-to-date with this is the Office for National Statistics. They run many surveys, including the Internet Access, Households and Individuals survey. Another report of note is the Internet Access Quarterly Update, taken from the Labour Force Survey. You can simply visit the ONS website to get the very latest reports.

Looking at the Internet Access Quarterly Update, you can learn more about Internet users themselves. For example, 82.3% of respondents have used the Internet at least once. When looking at age groups, you can see that over 95% of 18-44 have used the Internet before. You can also find that income levels do have a small impact on Internet usage. 90.8% of people earning less than £200 per week have ever used the Internet. This figure rises to 92.4% for those earning from £200 to £299 weekly, 95.1% for those earning £300 to £399, and to 96.4% for those £400 to £499. Another important fact to keep in mind is that 7.26 million of users are registered disable. Your site should be accessible to them as well as your abled users.

The Internet Access, Households and Individuals gives us a clearer insight into the habits of Internet users. The 2010 edition showed that 60% of Internet users connected everyday. The number of adults who had never used the Internet fell to 9.2 million in 2010, down from 10.2 million in 2009. The 2011 edition shows that mobile Internet is rising, with 45% of Internet users use their mobile phone to go online compared to 31% in 2010. The use of Wifi hotspots to connect has risen from 7% in 2010 to 13% in 2011. Home was still the most common place to connect to the Internet, being used by 95% of Internet users. The main use of the Internet is still to look for information about products and services, with 77% of Internet users citing this reason as a use. Social networking – using sites such as Facebook and Twitter – is now an important reason to use the Internet. 57% of users take part in this activity.

There is another important definition for your potential customers: they will be interested in your chosen subject. You will need to work out for yourself a profile of people that are interested in what you have to say and offer on your blog.

Start with media dealing with your subject. Specialist magazines, larger blogs and websites all may have already some data about their readers and visitors you may be able to use. Magazines usually have what is called a media kit. Inside is data – usually aimed at potential advertisers – that can help you define who reads the magazine, and thus is interested about the subject. Online publications – such as online magazines, websites and blogs – dealing with your subject will probably not help willingly. The larger websites and blogs may have their own media kits for you to use. Just pretend to be an advertiser.

Other ways to learn more about your potential readers is to ask your suppliers. If you have identified products and services that could be of interest to your readers, ask these providers for their own market research on their potential customers. It might be a question of chance

Internal Factors

whether or not you get access to this data. The large companies are not always willing to share this information. And small suppliers may not have much more than you when it comes to market research. But it is well worth the try. If you manage to get the data, it will allow you to pinpoint your own potential readers better. It is also a very good way to start a relationship with potential suppliers.

Once you have defined who in general is interested in your subject, you can work out how many of them are Internet users and thus can be reached by you. This will be your main target market.

Having identified your primary target market, nothing stops you from repeating the process in order to find secondary markets. Usually, these markets will be made up of people that closely relates to your primary market in terms of demographics. Your secondary markets could be a different age-group, people with a different education level, or those that could be interested in your blog for a totally different reason. Even gender could determine primary and secondary target markets.

For example, if your blog is about gaming you may find that men play video games more often than women. However, women players are increasing thanks to game producers targeting them specifically with some of their new titles. And so, it could become a viable market for you.

Your Blog as Your Product
As a blog publisher, you should remember that your website has two main reasons to be:

1. Satisfying your reader's needs or desires

2. Generating revenue for your business

It is important to keep this in mind when developing your blog in order to ensure success. Many people who decide to set up a blog just jump in without much preparations. This is fine if you only want to write for pleasure or to earn a small second income from your site. If you plan on making your blogging business a financial success, you need to spend some time defining your product strategy. This will be constructed around the key features of your blog. Your first job will be to identify these.

You should always focus on how your blog can benefit to your readers. Don't worry about what your blog does. Keep in mind what it does for your reader. Actually, most blogs have the same main key benefit: they provide information about a particular subject. Your aim should be to work out to offer the best information available. However, it is possible to find other benefits. This could be feeling better about oneself – in the case of a mind/body/spirit blog – or offering an added and/or specific benefit – such as exclusive stories and news, special discounts on products, competitions...

Many businesses are now trying to offer their customers additional value. Many products have attached to them additional, non-essential goods and/or services that often influence buyers. These can be money back guarantees, warranties, help and training to use, add-on products or services, accessibility... It is up to you to find what could be added to your particular blog to increase its value to your readers.

Place

In the marketing mix, place can be confusing. It will include everywhere you readers can find you, buy from you, and where you have control over what they read. This will also extend to how your products and information will be distributed to them.

Depending on your marketing plan, your readers could find you not only through your actual blog, but also your Twitter account, Facebook page, LinkedIn profile, and every other online publishing tools that you may decide to use. If you decide to extend extra services offline, it will also include your offices and any place you decide to meet clients in.

Your blog's distribution will rely entirely on your web hosting provider. The better hosting company you choose – or can afford – the better service you'll get. Nowadays, most hosting companies offer a service that will allow you to host a very simple blog without much trouble.

Internal Factors

Pricing

This is one of the most delicate aspect of the marketing mix. And even more so for a blogging business. Remember that the traditional way to blog is to offer readers information for free, and rely on advertising, and sales of related products – whether through affiliate marketing or by selling your own products. Unless you go through the effort of creating derivative products, you will not have to worry about pricing. But you should still know about it.

Pricing strategies can be varied. They will all impact on how your product – and by extension your business – is perceived by your customers. For example, when a product is the cheapest available, people will automatically assume that it is of lesser quality than the rest. But a range of people will still be attracted to it solely because of its price. A middle-priced product could be marketed as the best value for money – a compromise between price and quality. On the other hand, the most expansive product will automatically be viewed as a luxury item, and of very high quality. Its price, and its 'status' as a luxury item will attract a different kind of customers. These assumptions will then be tested by the customer. If they are satisfied that you did not lie to them, they may even buy again from you.

Of course, we have already noted that accessing a blog is usually free. You will need to convince people that you are offering them the best information available. And then you will need to convince them to buy by clicking links on your site so you can get your fee.

Promotion

Promoting your blog is a very important step. If people don't hear about you, they won't come to you either. Research has shown that people need to hear your name seven times before they buy from you. So you need think about how you will make your presence known.

This is also the time to clear up a common misconception. When most people hear the word promotion, they immediately think sales. From a marketing point of view however, promotion involves presenting your business and your products to people who can make the decision to buy, and those can influence that decision.

The tools of promotion include:

- advertising

- sales promotions

- direct sales

- public relations

Advertising is probably the most well-known promotional tool for businesses. As a blog, it is unlikely you will want to create a TV ad, or buy a series of display ads in a national newspaper – at least not when you start up. Most probably, you will focus on Internet advertising, and maybe local and/or specialist publications.

Sales promotions can be a very useful tool for blogs. Your readers will always be quite happy to receive discounts on the products your are recommending to them. It may also add value to your blog if you can secure exclusive discounts for your readers – that is, discounts that can't be found anywhere else.

In the case of a blog, **direct sales** can be defined as you contacting your readers rather than them coming to your site. Most direct selling you will conduct through your blog will probably happen through email marketing. As such, you must make sure you have a privacy policy in line with current anti-spam legislation, such as the Data Protection Act.

Public relations generally involves getting in touch with other media in order to get them talking about you. This could be getting reviews of your blog out, or attracting comments about your latest posts, Facebook presence, or Tweets. A simple presence in other media – even one very good review about one of your post – can be enough to bring your new readers. If your blog grows to be very successful, you may start to get enquiries from the press without you having to do anything.

People

You and any freelancers you employ to write for or manage a blog on your behalf will be very important. Remember that you are offering a service to your readers in the hope that they will then buy from or through you. If the information they receive is inaccurate, or the service sub-standard in any other way, there is very little chance they will come back to you, let alone buy anything.

If you decide to employ someone to help on your blog, make very sure they know what they are doing and give them clear instructions. You might also want to provide training as and when required. In the case of freelancers, you might want to talk with them about training them further by subsidizing their studies.

Process
Process describes the series of actions required to deliver your service and any other related products or services, to your customers' satisfaction. It will generally includes how you close your sales, distribute the product or service, and handle after-sales services, such as help desk and returns handling.

In your blog, you will be trying to sell products and services to your readers. Your style will define how you handle pre-sales advice. Distribution will be handled by whoever stocks the product. If you are concentrating on affiliate marketing, you will generally redirect your reader to another website. It will be their responsibility to close the sales, and handle after-sales.

However, if you decide to sell your own products, you will need to make these decisions for yourself. It is also important to remember your customers' expectations. In this day and age, most people have become impatient. If they order a digital product – such as an ebook, or video tutorial – they will expect this to be delivered straight away to them either via email or via a link on your blog. In the case of physical products, they will expect speedy delivery – a week at most for most goods.

Customer service – whether it is before, during or after the sale – is also vital to retain customers. You will need to develop a system to handle help queries, complaints, and returns. In the latter case, remember that customers are entitled to change their minds when ordering goods online. You will need to be able to give them refunds quickly and simply. You also need to put very strict guidelines in place for this. Some of the larger companies pay for all post and packaging involved in both sending a product and it being returned. Smaller businesses do not refund these fees when an order is returned to them. Whatever you decide, you will need to make sure your return conditions are clearly explained to your customers before they order anything from you.

Physical Evidences

In classical retail and manufacturing, this will often mean the labels and packaging attached to the products. For your blog, this will mostly mean your site's design. Although your product is the series of your posts, the way they are presented could make the difference between a returning reader, and one who never comes back.

Branding can be used to easily differentiate your blog – as well as your business – from others. Creating a brand could involve choosing a logo, colours, a slogan and/or name to define your blog. Although a blog does not have a traditional packaging, it is still a very visual product. Everything on your blog's pages and posts should appeal to your readers. This includes the colours you use in your design, the fonts you use for both text and headlines, and their sizes, the layout of your site...

If you are selling your own products, you could extend the concept to packaging. It doesn't need to be particularly fancy. A simple label bearing your logo, stuck on a plain package of white or brown can be all that's needed. You may also want to include some literature along with the products, such as related special offers, or even a simply invoice and thank you letter. Remember that the more your customers see of you, the greater the chances of them coming back to see what else you have to offer.

Your market research will help you to make a great many decisions that could influence the direction your blogging business takes. It is important to get it right, or you could find in an impasse within the first year, having spend hundred of pounds for your business and having seen absolutely no returns of any kind.

Checklist

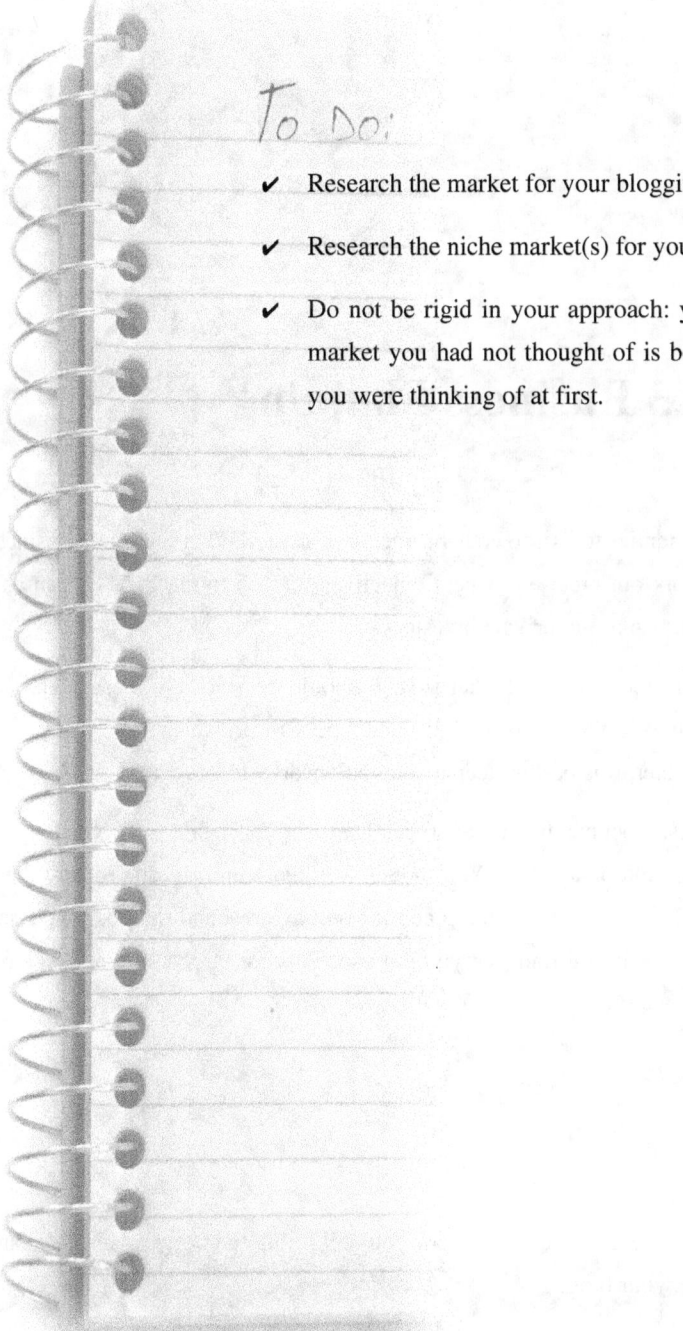

To Do:

✔ Research the market for your blogging business.

✔ Research the niche market(s) for your first blog.

✔ Do not be rigid in your approach: you may find that another market you had not thought of is better for you than the one you were thinking of at first.

2.3 Business Planning

There are two plans are essential tools for your business: your marketing and your business plans. They help you to work out precise business objectives for you to reach. They can also help to secure funding from banks and private investors.

Although we are presenting the marketing plan first, it should be said that these plans are better worked on at the same time. As you work on one, you will probably find information that will help defining the other. It is best to keep a notebook nearby to keep track of ideas.

Also keep in mind that these documents are not static. They are not meant to be written and stuffed in a drawer never to be look at again. You should keep them in mind and look at them regularly to see how your business is developing and if you have reached the goals you had set yourself. Revise your plans if you find that you fall short of your targets or that you have exceeded all your early expectations.

Your Marketing Plan

This plan will allow you to take a closer look at how you will promote both your business and your products – in our case, your blog.

Blog

Your Marketing Plan

Structure

Writing a marketing plan does not have to follow a strict structure, as does a business plan. However, there are a few things you really should write down in it in order to make it useful.

- ⏱ Purpose

- ⏱ Current Situation

- ⏱ Main Strategy and Objectives

- ⏱ Detailed Marketing Plan

- ⏱ Budgets, Time lines and Expected Results

Purpose

It is important for you to know why exactly you are creating this marketing plan. Of course, right now you are looking to introduce your blog to the wider world. But you could create an annual review plan, a plan to introduce new products into your blog, to promote a brand new blog, or even to start offering blogging services to other businesses.

You may also want to write down how your marketing plan ties in to your mission statement – if you have one. Although you may think that a mission statement is something big companies do in order to present themselves to the most inquisitive of their customers, it is also a very good way to focus your thoughts about your business and what you do through it. A mission statement is generally only a medium-sized paragraph.

Current Situation

You will already know most of the information you need to describe your situation, thanks to the previous chapter. Write it down now, presenting your blog, your potential readership, how your blog will be distributed, who your competitors are, what external forces are influencing the market, and what are your financial conditions.

Even if you are writing this plan for yourself, writing down everything about your situation will help you to formulate a strategy to better market your blog. A short summary of all this information might also be useful if you plan to present this plan to someone else in order to secure funding.

Main Strategy and Objectives

Your strategy, as a newly established blog, will involve developing your blog, finding new readers in your target market, and transforming these into regular users of your site. This will probably evolve as your blog grow. New strategies could be targeting a new market segment, developing new blogs, identifying emerging products for you to sell or promote...

Once you have established your strategy, you should set yourself one or more business goals. When doing this, you should remember to keep these objectives achievable within the parameters of your time, resources, and budget. If you have already decided on a very small marketing budget, it is unlikely you will find 100,000 new readers in the space of six months.

> **Tip:**
>
> Have a small brainstorming session to see how many ideas you can come up with by yourself. Don't cheat and don't look at the marketing chapter. This will allow you to find out if you are creative enough to handle your marketing yourself. If can't think up more than five ideas, no problem. We'll give you some help later on. But you might want to look for either a marketing agency willing to work on a performance basis, or even a business partner with marketing experience or a creative mind.

Detailed Marketing Plan

This is where you will explain, step by step, what you intend to do to promote your blog. There are four key areas for which you must make marketing decisions for your blog:

- ☺ Your markets – Of course, in a start up marketing plan, you main objective will be to penetrate your primary target market. However, as you grow, you may decide to reach secondary markets that you will have identified during market research.

- ☺ Your product – In a start up plan, you will want to explain what your primary product will be (your blog and its niche subject), what it can offer your potential readers, what it will look like and why. When expanding your business, you also want to say how you plan to change your product to increase sales – whether changes come in the form of new topics to write about, new design, new features, or anything else that deals with the blog itself.

- Marketing tools – This is where you explain at length how you will promote your blog. How will you use the four areas of promotion: advertising, public relations, direct selling, and sales promotions? What will your objectives be? What about your main messages and themes? We discuss marketing tools in more details in further chapters.

- Distribution – How will you distribute your content to your users? How will you make sure your content is always available? What are the costs involved?

- Market research – How will you keep track of your readers' needs and wants? Do you outsource it, or keep it in-house? Remember that the Internet has millions other sources of information. As soon as you stop delivering what they want, your readers will go looking elsewhere.

There are an additional two areas you should keep in mind, although they will not always apply to your blog.

Pricing is often an important part of a good marketing strategy. Blogs are usually free to access, and as such pricing is not a real consideration. It may become one if you are planning to sell your own products, advertising space, or even transform your blog in a membership site. In which case, you will have to decide how much to charge for your products and/or services. Your prices will need to cover all your business costs, while giving a good pricing margin. You will also need to be careful what your competitors are charging. If you charge too much more, your readers will go to them because they are cheaper. Charge too little, and many will go to your competitor because they will perceive you as 'not as good'. It's a difficult balancing act, and you need to carefully track results, as the slightest change in strategy can spell great success or total disaster.

Customer service is the last thing you should consider. Although you might think it has nothing to do with marketing, it impacts hugely on what people think of you and so on what they will go and say to their friends and family about your blog – and that's word-of-mouth marketing. So how will you keep your readers happy with what you have to offer? How can they contact you if they have a complaint? Or even just a question? How quickly will you respond to these?

Budgets, Time lines and Expected Results

This should show time constraints, budgets if you have any, and the results you are realistically hoping to achieve. Remember not to be too optimistic when drafting your very first marketing plan. Unless you have already used the marketing techniques to promote a similar business, you have no real idea how well a promotional tool will work until you put it into practice. You should also keep in mind that when it comes to blogging, what works with one sites may not work with another one. Marketing blogs is a process of trial and error.

Your Business Plan

A business plan is a tool with two main aims: raise funds to start or expand a business, and monitor your business targets in order to measure success. A business plan should also be tailored to its readers.

Structure

There are more ways of writing a business plan than there are banks around the world. The following is just the one we find the most effective, and the easiest to adapt to external requirements.

- ⏰ Executive Summary

- ⏰ Markets and Competitors

Your Business Plan

- Your Business and Product

- Yours and Your Team's Skills

- Marketing Plan

- Operational Plan

- Financial Forecasts

- Annexes

Let's have a more detailed look at each section...

Executive Summary

This should actually be the very last part you write, although it is the first thing any potential investor will look at. As the name indicates, it should give a general idea of your entire business plan in one or two pages. Work on it long and hard, as it could be the only thing a busy business angel reads before making the decision to invest or not.

It should at least contain a general description of your business, products and services, a quick overview of your market and where you fit into it, your mission statement – your business objectives and ideology – and if the plan is meant to raise funds, how much you require altogether, how much you already have and from where, and how much you'd like from the people reading the plan.

Your Market and Competitors

In this part, you should present your industry, your market(s) and your competitors. This is where most of the market research you have done in the previous chapter will come in very handy.

You will need to present this data to someone who may have absolutely no idea about blogging as a business. Consequently, you should try to keep the jargon down to a minimum.

If you have to use it, make sure you explain it in writing as you may not have the chance to do this in person.

If potential investors do not believe that there is potential in this market after reading this, it is unlikely they will loan you any funds. So make sure that your figures are water-tight. Resist the temptation to play with the numbers, whatever happens. Any savvy investors will quickly spot this and you will loose their trust, and thus their money.

Your Business and Product

Here comes the first part about your blog. It is probable that your blog will be both your business and your product as you start. Or you could decide to keep both firmly separate as you aim to develop more blogs, or launch other internet publishing ventures. If you decide to present your blog as your product – as opposed to your business – make sure to present your business first, then your blog.

Present your Unique Selling Point. Explain what will make your blogging business and your blog different from the others. Your USP could be pretty much anything. Widely used claims for blogs are offering the best deals on the Internet, bringing the very latest news, and being the acknowledged expert on a particular subject. The more unique your approach, the better you will be able to compete.

This is also the place to present your SWOT analysis. During market research, you have analysed your competitors Strengths and Weaknesses. It is now time to find out what are yours. Opportunities and Threats will have been identified during your PESTEL analysis. Your aim over the next few years in business should be to transform your weaknesses into strengths, to take advantage of existing opportunities and work so threats are eliminated whenever possible or at least carefully monitored. It might even be possible to transform some of them into new opportunities.

Your SWOT analysis allows potential investors to see that you have thought things through and are being realistic about your situation. It will also allows you to see exactly where you stand what you should work on – thus allowing you to develop better marketing and business plans. Be honest when doing this exercise.

Your Business Plan

As we have already seen, your product will be your blog. You will need to present it further here: its subject, monetization model(s). It is also a good idea to remind investors here of your target market(s). If you are looking to build different income streams, explain what and how. This is also the time to explain your blog's USP, philosophy, branding, and any other differentiation you have planned. The whole point here is to explain why you think people will come to read your blog, and why they will come back for more information.

Yours and Your Team's Skills

Describes what make you qualified to run this blogging enterprise. Remember that we are not just talking about blogging here. Potential investors will also want to know if you can run the business.

Note down any experience you have that will qualify you for running a blogging business. This could be experience in your chosen niche, experience as a blogger – whether on a personal or professional blog – experience in management, experience running your own business...

Also explain what training – if any – you have already received or plan to get. The Prince's Trust can offer free business training to under thirty years olds living in the UK. Alternatively, your local branch of Business Link or your Chamber of Commerce could put you in touch with good training providers. Some might even be able to find you a business mentor.

Once you have provided these details about yourself, repeat the process about each member of your team, whether they work for you full or part time or are freelancers.

Marketing Plan

This part should explain briefly what decisions you have made when it comes to marketing your business and your blog. If you have a detailed marketing plan – as the one you would have created if you followed our marketing plan advice – put in the appendices. Here you should just sum up what you intend to do to promote the business. Time lines, marketing goal and budgets are not important.

Simply present the basic elements of your marketing mix: Product, Price, Promotion, Place, People, Process and Physical Evidence. Remember that you will need to show both how you will attract new readers and how you will convert them into buying customers. Your final profits will be in direct relation to this conversion rate.

Operational Plan

This show how you will run your blogging operation. You may have already introduced a few facts when you introduced your business – such as your chosen legal structure, and whether you will be working from home or intend to rent premises. You should present these again, and add considerably to these facts.

Here, you will basically present how your business will be run on a daily basis. Every aspect of your blogging business should appear here. As a broad guideline, you should mention the following:

- Business basics – As mentioned above, your legal structure, place of work, amount tied in premises (if renting/leasing/buying) as well as the length of the agreement, business insurances in place, and how you will handle day-to-day activities such as book-keeping and purchasing.

- Production – You need to put systems in place to handle basic blogging activities such as researching, writing, editing, and posting entries on your site. You also need to keep track of related expenses such as web hosting, freelance writers and editors if you employ any, and how these perform for your business. What systems have you put in place to assure of the quality of the final products?

- Marketing – How will you implement the ideas you have developed through your marketing plan. Do not explain what you will do, just how you will do it. If you decide to employ affiliate marketing tactics, how will you track the results of your affiliates? If you employ a freelance Internet marketer to help with SEO and blog and forum posting, how will you track their results?

- Distribution – How will your blog and related products or services be distributed? Where will they be sold? What deals have you already put in place with suppliers? How will you ensure their reliability? Have you put in place stock control and fulfilment systems if you are selling your own physical goods?

- Customer Service – How will you make sure your customers are satisfied? What systems have you put in place to handle complaints and returns? If you employ someone to handle part or all of customer service, how will you know if they are efficient for your business?

Financial Forecast

This is the part that investors will really based their decisions on. Any unrealistic fact or prediction here will amount to your business plan being turned down for funding. So take the time to get it right.

Make a note of how much funding you need in total, and how much has already been raised by you. If you can offer any type of security – such as house, car, office equipment, or anything else you can think of – let your potential investors know. Remember that if you offer these security, you will loose the item in question if you fail to repay the loan.

There are four statements your investors will want to see:

- Income Sources – Where is your money coming from. We have already explored the potential income streams for a blog. Now you need to explain this to your investors.

- Sales Forecast – This is how much you expect to sell over the first year of your business. Remember to research and include any sales patterns. For example, retail businesses often see increase sales during the few months leading up to Christmas. This is usually followed by a slow January and maybe even February as customers have less to spend then. Find out if your niche has similar selling patterns you can exploit.

- Cashflow Forecast – This will show month by month, how much you expect to earn and spent over the space of your first year in business. Most investors will request forecasts for anything between twelve and thirty-six months depending on how much you want to borrow from them. It can also be useful to come up with two scenarios for your first year trading: a reasonable projection, and a worst case scenario.

🕐 Profit and Loss Forecast: This will show at a glance what profit you expect to make. Remember that breaking even, even making a loss is acceptable during your first year. But you need to show you have what it takes to turn that situation into healthy profits within three years.

Appendices

Many things can end up in this part of your business plan: detailed market research, your full-length marketing plan, resumes of all the people involved in your business, examples of your stationery and other branding, advertising you are planning to use, sample posts from your blog... More is not necessarily better, but anything that may help your case could find a home here.

Raising Funds

With the two plans above, you are ready to approach potential investors. Money is the lifeblood of any business. You will need some to start up, and probably some more to grow your business. How much depends on what you need to buy. Luckily, a blogging business has low starting costs and overheads.

Your business plan should give your potential investors all the information they need to make an informed decision about lending you any money. You should also remember that there are various ways to secure the funding you need.

Raising Funds

Invest your own money

It is highly unlikely that anyone will offer you finance if you are not prepared to risk your own money in your business venture. In most cases, you will be required to finance at least half of your business's starting costs.

Friends and Family

If someone you know has some money going spare, they can be a better way for you to secure funds than any financial institution. Show them your business plan, and give them a copy. They will then know exactly where their money goes and how you expect to pay them back. Acquaintances and relatives are likely to offer zero-interest loans to you. They may also be far more flexible when it comes to repayment terms. However, if you fail to repay them, this could easily strain your personal relationship.

If your friend also happen to be knowledgeable – blogging or business-wise, you could actually set up a partnership of some kind rather than ask for a loan. It would allow your friend to profit more from the business. It could also mean the workload gets split rather than you doing all the work.

If they decide to help, whichever way, seek advice from a financial advisor and draw up a proper contract. This should protect every party involved.

Banks

They usually are the first source of funding entrepreneurs turn to. They have the advantage of being able to offer both loans and overdraft facilities. However, banks will often require some type of security before agreeing to fund a business. So if you do not keep up with the repayments, you may loose whatever you have used as security. They will also look at your credit history and business track record. Of course, as a start up your business will not have a record, so your own credit history may count for double.

It has been difficult to secure bank funding over the recession. But it is not impossible either, if your business plan is solid enough. If you meet all requirements to obtain a loan from a bank, but lack a good security, you may be eligible for the Small Business Loan Guarantee

Scheme. This government-backed scheme can provide security for up to 70% of your loan. If your loan is small enough, this could easily be secured on the computer equipment you will use for your blog.

Grants & Government Support

Generally, the government can offer financial support to small businesses. These can take the forms of cash grants, 0% or low-interest loans and/or security to get access to bank funding. Most of the schemes are administered by a third party and come with stringent criteria. These can be working for a particular industry, or spending the money in a particular way. The review process, to both obtain the money, and prove that you have spent it the way you should, can make the whole affair a real headache.

> **Tip:**
>
> There is another type of funding for business: venture capital. Usually, this is only available to business with high growth potential. Although also available to qualifying start ups, it is unlikely you will secure this type of funding for a start up blogging business. You may be able to secure this as you expand your business though.

Competition is also very, very tough. You will probably have to compete with hundreds of other business from across your region, sometimes even the country or Europe, for a chance at getting the money. This is particularly true now, when bank funding has shrunk rather dramatically despite the promises of our governments. You need a very good case to win grant funding.

The best way to find out about what grants and loans are available to you is to visit the Business Link website. They have an easy to use database. Answer a few question about what you do, and why you need the money, and they'll match you with the most likely sources of funding for you.

Finding Support

Working for yourself is a big challenge. But you don't have to go at it entirely alone. They are plenty of people who are willing to help, whether you need advice within the blogging industry, or more wide ranging business help.

Blogging Advice

You will find that quite a few people are willing to help newcomers to develop their own blogs. Of course, those you are in direct competition with – bloggers with the same niche as yours or one closely related – might not be as forthcoming. But many still help if you can help them in return. Building contacts in the industry is probably the best way to learn. But there are other ways...

There are plenty of blogs about blogging. If you want to learn about the latest news in the industry, this is the best way to go. The most read blog about the subject might be ProBlogger. They boast a readership of more than 300,000. They also publish a series of books on how to build better blogs as well as offer a community where you can start making useful contacts. Other blogs you might want to investigate are Copyblogger and DailyBlogTips.

WarriorForum is another place to make many useful contacts. Although focused on Internet marketing rather than blogging, these forums are still great to find advice as well as products to promote on your site. You can also find opportunities for ready-made sites and blogs, to get early reviewers, and find some professional help for your Internet marketing efforts. If your products and services fit the niche of Internet marketers, you can offer them to the other members.

Software communities are another place where to find very useful help and advice. Most CMS and blogging platforms have their own forums. They serve mainly as a support network for the actual platform. Once you have chosen your blogging platform, you will find that most also host forums and maybe even blogs to help out new comers. It is often a good idea to sign up on these and ask the senior members for help when you run into troubles. They will most probably be suing the same platform as you and thus will be experienced in using it. However, you may still be able to use some of the sections to make useful contacts in the industry. Just be mindful of any rules about advertising and linking within the forums.

Business Advice

Starting a business is difficult. However, there are many places to go to get some help. As soon as you have put together the basis of your marketing and business plans, find your local Business Link office and ask what they can do for you. From training opportunities to finding a business mentor or some funding, there are many ways they could help. You can also get advice on their website.

Your local Chamber of Commerce may also have some very good resources you can make use of. As well as providing you with a networking opportunity in your region, they may offer training and advice. Although some of their services are reserved to members, it is also possible for non-members to access some of their offers by paying a premium fee.

Do not under-estimate the powers of your local community, and your local business professionals in particular. Your accountant may well become your favourite person. As well as saving you money on your taxes, they may know just the business you are looking to work with, whether they need your services or you need theirs. Your solicitor can also be useful. If you manage to find one with a good working knowledge of the online publishing industry, they will know other businesses in the industry. If you use a small broker to secure your insurances, it may be helpful to them and your to exchange a few business cards. They may push business your way, and you might just be able to return the favour.

Many places run small business networking events, over breakfast or a cup of coffee. Even if you do not intend to blog for others at first, it can be a good idea to establish whether local small business would be interested in using these services. Making these contacts early can give you the edge in terms of finding funding to expand if necessary.

Checklist

To Do:

✔ Research and write your marketing and business plans

✔ Work out how you will fund your business. A blogging business has low starting costs and overheads. But it will take 3 to 6 months before you start to even break even

✔ Create a support network for your business. Contact Business organisation, training programmes, Chamber of Commerce, and local businesses who may become your suppliers. You should also ask friends and family if they can help in any way - maybe spreading word-of-mouth, or handling the school runs.

3 – Starting up

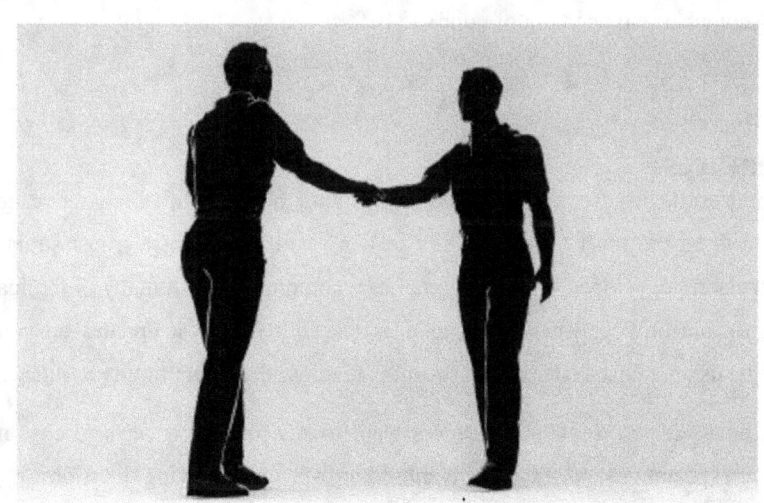

3.1 Setting Up Your Blog

Now that you have done your research, you are ready to actually start your blog itself. There still are many decisions to be made in order to have the best first blog possible for your business. The simplest way to get it right the first time around is to take the time to write down precisely what you need out of your site before you start building it.

Blog Features

It is important to decide from the start what it is your blog will do for your readers. Some blogs decide to be the most basic they can be – no bells and whistles, just straightforward content. Others are developed to have the feel of a community, with many of the features you can expect to find on social networks, such as the ability to post updates on your profile. Others will be using a chat system and/or forums to allow their community to interact.

Depending on what you think your readers want to see, there are ways to customize your blogs to their expectations. As a start, you should answer the following questions:

- Media types – What media will your users prefer to see on your blog? Articles, mini-posts, pictures, audio, video, all of the above?

Blog Features

- ⏱ Features – What will your users want to do/use while on your site? Forums, email access, user profiles, social network, mini-games... All can be implemented with a little of preparation.

> **Tip:**
>
> Multi-media blogs are fast becoming favourites with both users and search engines. It can be worth the effort.

- ⏱ Organization – How will your posts be organized? What broad categories will you use? What about tags? And what of the few informational static pages of your blog (such as 'about us', 'contact us', 'privacy policy', 'terms and conditions'...)? How will your users access these?

Hosting

You probably have already looked around at a number of service providers when it comes to hosting. Before making your final decision, you should take into account the choices you have made above. If you are looking for some very peculiar features, some hosted services may not be able to accommodate you.

Some web hosting plans offer only the very basics in terms of bandwidth and space. Blogs created with dedicated software are generally take only a small amount of web space. However, you may need more if you have decided to build a multi-media blog – in particular if you are using videos. You should also take into account how fast you expect your blog to grow. If you already have a lot of content planned or if you expect your readership to grow rapidly, make sure your hosting service can easily grow with you.

The same can apply with certain other hosting features, such as email boxes, FTP access, databases... For example if you want to offer your users the possibility of creating their own blog from yours, and an email address associated with your domain name, you will need to make sure your hosting company can provide all of this. There are some very nice features to have, although they may not be essential. One-click installation software – such as Fantastico and QuickInstall – can make it very simple to create a blog. Choosing a hosting service that offers an uptime guarantee is particularly important. This guarantee will ensure that your

Tip:

Domain add-ons allow you to create multiple websites on one account. If your account also includes unlimited webspace and bandwidth and a number of databases, you could host several small readership blogs without any problem.

website is available to your readers most, if not all, of the time. You need to make sure that any downtime does not disturb your business too much. If your readers are experiencing too much errors because of busy servers, you will lose them to rival sites or media outlets.

Other very nice features when looking to start any kind of online business is free vouchers for online advertising. Some can offer you up to $400 worth of free advertising with your hosting account. However, not all these companies are reliable when it comes to uptime, and some have poor customer service. Always research your web host before signing up. Just look for reviews and complaints by other users. You will then need to decide which reviews are honest, and which are just from people being upset at the company.

Although it is not that difficult to migrate to a new hosting provider, it might be time consuming, result in lost traffic and sales whilst your domain name is redirected to the new server(s), and you could well loose data if you forgot to back up or something went wrong when you did. Some companies do offer to help you transfer your site over, for a price. However, it might be best to choose right the first time around.

Name and Domain Name

During your brainstorming session, you might have hit on the perfect name for your blog. It is best to keep it short and simple for your users to remember. You can now look for a domain name. This is where you might find that your chosen name as already been taken. Remember that although .com is by far the most used, it is not the only domain extension. If you absolutely want a particular name, and can't get the .com, the .net, .biz, .org or .info might still be available. Country-tied extensions – such as .co.uk, .fr, .de – can also be used, but remember it implies ties to that particular country.

Name and Domain Name

If all domain extensions are taken or you want a particular one, you may be able to buy the domain name off its current owner. This option may not be simple, in particular if the current owner is from a different country and does not speak English. The negotiation could also be very long and you may end up paying more for the domain name than for the rest of your business.

The simplest way is to come up with a different name. In order to make the whole process a bit quicker, you could use the domain name checks that many web hosting companies offer. They will let you know if your new name is already taken and may also offer a few choices for alternative names.

Brainstorming

The first thing you should do is sit down with pen and paper and have a brainstorming session. This will help you to clarify your goals and find your first few ideas for content. It can also influence what your site will look like, what features it will have, its name, what platform you will end up using, what hosting solution will be best for you and your site...

The best way to brainstorm is to have a white page. Write your chosen niche in the centre of the page. Then set a timer – or your phone's alarm – for five to ten minutes, and write down all the ideas you have for your site. There are several ways to keep the ideas coming: mind-mapping where you create a diagram where all ideas relate to each others on your paper; word associations, which can be particularly good to find content ideas; free writing can help you to think up really original ideas for your design, branding, content – and pretty much everything else... If you do get stuck, it is sometimes a good idea to have your market research nearby to have a look at. It might give you a few more ideas and starting points to write during your session.

If you prefer to have some guidelines to help your session, you can always divide your paper – or get several more pages – and write down the main things you need to find for your site: content, design, branding/marketing ideas, features, navigation items and the different sections of your site, your main keywords...

After you have finished a brainstorming session, it is always a good idea to put the results aside for a little while. Come back to it with fresh eyes and you might find that new ideas jump at you from the pages. Another good way to make the most of your session is to get a few friends together to help you come up with new ideas.

Choosing Your Platform

Your dream platform will ideally have many of the features you are looking for, either within the core system or by adding plugins or add-ons. However, you should not just choose a platform because they claim to be the best, the most user-friendly, or the one used by millions of others. Make sure you choose the one that is right for you and your site!

Is it easy enough for you to use, or at least learn? Most CMS and blogging platforms are user friendly, but they all have their very own interface. It's up to you to see if you feel comfortable using that interface on a regular basis. If not, then it might be best to choose another platform for your blog. You need to remember that you will be spending a lot of time uploading content to your blog(s). The process must be simple and easy to you, or you will be loosing valuable time struggling with your software instead of developing your business.

How much support is available for this platform? Many open source platforms – such as WordPress and Drupal – will offer support from the community through the forums on their websites. If you decide to use a paid-for services, you may well be able to get help from your provider during business hours.

How easy is it to extend the core system? If no blogging platform offers everything you require from a simple installation, you will need to extend these functionalities with modules. These are variously called plugins, add-ons, extensions, modules, or any other similar name. What you need to find out is how easy these will be to install onto your site. Are you required to play with some code? Or will they work straight out of the box?

How easy is it to design your site around the core system? You might think this question irrelevant, in particular if you will be buying a template from a freelance designer, or an agency. However, it is important to think about this. In all likelihood, you will want to change

Choosing Your Platform

your site's design – maybe to accommodate a new branding, to reflect a change in management or direction, to mark particular holidays, or simply because the previous one was not working as well as you thought it would. The question will be, can you afford to pay a designer each time you want to make the simplest of modifications to your site? If not, does your blogging platform allow you to change your design easily? Do you need to learn the basics of coding? Or is there a drag and drop system you can use?

How much will it cost you? You should not think only in terms of money when answering this question. Remember that your time is also very valuable. If you are desperately bad with computers, might it be worth it to invest into a paid-for system offer more support than community forums? If you can't design a good looking website, might it be better to get someone in who can do a good job in the space of a few hours or days?

Does it have, or can it get, most if not all of the features you want? Let us start by saying that if a blogging platform does not have everything you need, then you should not be using it. When it comes to the features you want, it is slightly different. Your first stop should be the extension page on your chosen platform's website. From there, you should be able to establish whether or not the platform can do what you want it to. You should also stop by the forums to see which extensions work better than others, whether there are alternatives to paid extensions that work as well, and if the developer is actively trying to resolve the problems as they are discovered by the users.

The best way to find the platform of your dreams is still to try it out. Don't believe what you are told in tutorials and video presentation. Find a cheap – or free – web host, and install your top three platforms. Play around with the content management system, post a few sample posts and pages, have a look how installing a ready-made template or designing one from scratch works. Only then will you be able to choose.

Get the Design Right

It is important to create a design for your visitors that is easy to understand and use, and that will reflect the subject of your site in some way. Many of the following tips may seem common sense, but it is a good idea to keep them firmly in mind when shopping around for a design, or talking with your web designer.

Colours

If you have already worked out a branding identity for your site – and maybe created a logo to go with it – it is a good idea to carry through the colours of that identity to the rest of your web design. The Internet is mostly a visual medium. And your visitors will use your logo and colour scheme to identify your site.

It is also important to remember that some colours will be associated to certain subjects or emotions in the mind of your audiences. And these associations may vary wildly between your audiences and their cultural background. It is a good idea to research these potential associations before you decide on your colour scheme – including choosing the colours of your logo.

Navigation

This is a very important element of your design as it will allow your visitors to use your site. A good navigation will help your visitor to use your site to its maximum potential. And ease of use may well mean returning readers in the long run.

Navigation elements have long since found their preferred place in website design. There are two main positions that are used:

- Top – either right at the top of the design, or just below the header elements where you usually find the title and/or logo of the blog;

- Sides – Left and right sidebars are also often used to present some navigational elements such as the archives, or links to social networks.

Get the Design Right

The arrival of widgets as also seen footers being used to present navigational links, such as links to the top of the page and/or the home page, breadcrumbs, and links to register to the site and to log in.

You need to work out where best to put these elements in order to make your blog as simple to use as possible.

Finding Themes, Templates, Frameworks, or Freelancers

There are many places on the Internet where you can find some ready-made templates for your sites. When looking to buy one, you should keep in mind one important thing: you're not necessarily shopping for the design, but the framework it comes built into.

Most templates will be built around a CMS or will come in pure HTML/CSS. Places such as Dream Templates, ThemeForest, or TemplateMonster can provide you with read-made templates for your chosen CMS. Templates can simply be downloaded to your computer, then uploaded to your server and installed – all in the space of thirty minutes. If you decide to buy an HTML/CSS design, it will involve a bit more work to integrate the design within your CMS. You might want to use an extension to make this easier, or pay someone to do the job. You should remember that if some design elements do not fit with your view of what your site should look like, you can always change them to match your ideal site more closely.

Frameworks are a great tools if you have a very precise idea of what your site should look like. They can allow you to design your site down to the last details, while using a set of tools that allow to cut down on the designing time. WordPress frameworks, in particular, have been developed to be particularly powerful. For example, the Genesis framework is one of the most used WordPress framework. Several child themes are available for it, and you can also use it to develop themes for others.

There is always the alternative to find some help from a professional. There are many places online, such as oDesk and Freelancer.com where you might be able to find some freelance designers. They can design your blog around the platform you have chosen and the features you have implemented – or are planning to implement.

To Do:

✔ Research the features your blog needs to stand up to the competition.

✔ Plan out a basic design on paper before you go online.

✔ Choose a web host and a blogging platform.

✔ Install the barebones of the system, and set it all up.

✔ Work out design issues: navigation, colour, graphic elements, and integration of the features within the design.

3.2 Content

The saying 'Content is king' holds very true with blogging. The better your content, the more people will come to your site for information about your niche. The one thing that should be noted is that you do not need to create the entirety of your content. There are many sources of ready-made content for you to use around the Internet. Just remember to respect the copyright of others as you would like them to respect yours.

Researching Content

Of course, before you can start to post to your newly created blog, you need to know what you will appear on it. It is possible that you will already have lots of ideas for content. However, you will need to develop a system to keep the ideas flowing. Remember that in order to keep people returning to your blog, you will need to provide loads of content over the year. It will need to be informative, of good quality, and not too repetitive or your readers will get bored.

Content Sources

Your market research is the first thing you should look at when looking for ideas. If you are doing your job right – even long after your blog has been launched – your market research will tell you who your readers are and what they want out of your blog. It's up to you to deliver. This is another reason to keep in touch with your readers beyond reading and responding to their comments. You could use a blog post to ask them what they want to learn more about. You could also run a survey now. SurveyMonkey could help you to run surveys for a low cost.

You should obviously follow the news pertinent to your niche. Newspapers, magazines, radio, TV programmes, and other blogs can all be part of your news network. If you make contacts with suppliers in the field, you might be able to report on their news as and when they happen. Another source of news are press release distribution services such as PRweb and PrLog. Press and news releases can be used as the basis for your own posts. All the companies using these services are hoping for this: that bloggers and journalists will pick up on their stories and follow up with a post or article. To create content this way requires some more research, and maybe a quick phone call to get more details on the story. But it can create contacts with potential suppliers and advertisers, as well as give you content that other bloggers may have missed – giving you exclusivity.

Content ideas

To create a list of everything you could ever write about would take far too long. More to the point, too many of the ideas would be totally irrelevant to your chosen niche. However, there are a few things that will work for pretty much every blog:

- Interviews – From experts in the field or suppliers with new products, interviews will generally bring fresh content to your blog, and interesting points of views to your readers.

- Reviews – This is another idea that is used often enough in blogs. Find a product and present your review of it. Of course, it is up to you if your focus is to sell said product, or present an unbiased opinion of the strengths and weaknesses of said product.

- Tutorials – Whether it comes in the form of a few tips and advice on a particular feature or process, a more general introduction product or software, or a very detailed walk-through, tutorials are very useful to your readers. As such, they usually do well as content.

- News reporting – This is essentially what any journalist would do. Find a story and report it happening. It works with blogging as well. You can report on new products, services, what's happening in the industry... What you really want is exclusive stories – where you are the first to report them and everyone else is just a follower. These can be difficult to find when starting up, but if you build your contacts well enough, you could find these stories soon enough. Of course, you can create your own news as well. If your blog has just reached the 10,000 visitors mark, or anything else, you can blog about it!

- Opinion pieces – Your readers are interested in your point of view as well as the news. Create content citing other people's blog posts or blog comments. Link back to a newspaper's article you read, or a piece of news you heard on the radio. And then say what you think about it all. This content idea works best when your point of view is very different from that of the original piece.

Keyword Research

You may wonder what keywords have to do with your content. If you know a bit about SEO, you will know that keywords play an important part in helping to organise your content for search engines. They will also help your site to achieve a better ranking on search results for these keywords. As such, you should research relevant keywords for your content at the same time as you are researching it.

Google has a good number of tools to help you research keywords, such as the Google Adwords keyword tools, Google Insight, and Google Trends. They can all help you to choose your keywords wisely if you are heavily relying on Google search engine. If you also receive traffic via other search engines, then supplementing the tools above with WordTracker and/or WordStream could be a good idea. These tools will help you to choose the best keywords for your current post. They can also tell you what your readers want to learn more about. Many people just go to their favourite search engine and type in keywords to find content. This is where looking at the history of the searches can be important. If the keyword is constantly searched, maybe you should create content around it more often. If a keyword is only searched at certain times of the year, have content ready when the search numbers start to rise again.

If you are going to write some content – or have it written for you – it is also important to know in advance which keywords should be used within your post. Keyword density refers to the number of times your chosen keywords appear in your text. Although only a very small part of SEO, it can be useful to get this rig1ht. Many experts consider the 3% mark to be optimum for keyword density. If you'd rather not count your keywords in each post or article you write, try KeywordDensity.com or KeywordDensityTools.com.

Content Formats

Once you know *what* you will blog about, you can decide which content format to present your content in. Search engine have learned to love multi-media websites.

Word Content

This form of content is still the most used on blogs. This could be because blogs were originally created with articles in mind. Your writing style will have to become your own, but we can give you some tools to make writing articles, press release and other 'word content' more quickly and efficiently.

There are several things you can do with words:

- posts

- articles

Content Formats

- special reports

- books/ebooks

Video Content

Video are now very big on the Internet. They are used to create tutorials, offer some tips and advice, present products and services... Whatever you put in an article, you could easily make a video for it. The best run time for blog videos stands between two and five minutes. It allows you to say what you want to, and let your readers get on with the rest of their day quickly. Remember that time is a precious commodity nowadays.

Keep your readers' attention by telling them what the video is about straight away. Don't keep back information. As mention above, your reader's time is limited. They want to gain a lot from your site, quickly.

There are three main types of video on the Internet nowadays: the talking head, the slide show, and the screen capture.

- Talking head video is the name given to those videos where you simply talk to your readers. The only things needed to create one of these are a good quality web cam and a good script. These can be very effective when offering tips and advice as they feel more personal to your readers.

- A slide video can effectively be created from a programme such as PowerPoint. Create a series of slides showing off your content, add some nice fade in/out or slide effects, and you have a video. These can be good for presentation of new products or services. Animoto and SpotMixer are two very good services for this.

- Screen capture video allows you to do just that: capture whatever happens on your screen and turn it into a video. These videos have become very popular to present computer-related tutorials. Jing, Camtasia and CamStudio are all good software to work with.

Audio Content

Although audio content is not often used as stand-alone content on blogs, nothing stops you from creating purely audio posts if you want to. This can be particularly useful for interviews. It allows your readers to hear both you and your interviewee, and can help build relationships.

A simple microphone is all you need to make a recording at your computer. When going out to interview someone, a good digital recorder can make your life a lot easier when it comes to transferring the recording to your computer. Alternatively, your phone may have a recording feature. It is also possible to use the likes of Skype and FreeConferenceCalling to record interviews when your subject lives on the other side of the world.

Whatever your chosen way of recording, you will need to make sure the final files are either MP3s or WAVs. These two file formats are now the norm. If you want to save yourself some bother, you can use software such as MP3-recorder, MP3AudioRecorder, and MP3 My MP3. These will allow you to record in MP3 formats.

Webinars

Webinars are very useful in a wide variety of ways. The main opportunities they can offer a blogging business relate to creating long lasting relationships with your readers and potential customers. They can be used to offer training, present a new service or product live, even to hold a conference about a particular aspect of your niche. The best online tool remains GoToMeeting. However, TokBox and Freebinar can be very useful to smaller bloggers as they are free webinar services.

Content Sourcing and Creation

There are plenty of ways to source content on the Internet. From this content, you can research your own, or simply re-distribute the content you find.

Content Sourcing and Creation

<table>
<tr><td>

Tip:

Search engines do not really like duplicated content. You can have some on your site, but most of your content must be unique. To avoid losing your rank in search results, aim to have no more than 10% duplicated content on your site.

</td></tr>
</table>

Article directories

There is an endless amount of content within article directories. More often than not, these directories will store articles that you can copy and re-use on your own site for free. The only requirement is to keep all links within the article 'live', that is pointing to the place the author decided on. This is generally their own website, or a place where to buy their products and/or services.

If you are worried about duplicated content bringing your site ranking down, there is always the option of using the articles found on directories as research for your own. The best article directories remain GoArticles, EzineArticles, Squidoo, and eHow.

Article Spinners

If you are looking to create unique content very quickly from an article you have already created, then this type of tool is for you. An article spinner – also called article re-writer – will do just that. It will re-write your content, changing words here and there, to make a 'new' article from your previous one. Not all article spinners work as well as each other. It can be a bit of a trial and error until you find the one you really like. We can recommend the following software though:

ContentProfessor – This tool is web-based, and as such perfect if you are working away from the office. You can use it for free. Some features will be limited, such as only being able to save one article at a time. However, it can create a large number of articles with one click of a button. You will find a small selection of articles on the site for you to use as your own.

KillerContentSystem – This is actually a membership site. It will give you access to a constantly updated database of articles for you to spin your content from.

Guest Bloggers

Finding guest bloggers is a good way of getting content for your site without having to write it. There is still a lot of work involved though. You will need to make contacts with other bloggers in your niche or some closely related ones. Most bloggers will be happy to guest blog for you if you return the favour or help their own blog somehow.

Usually, guest blogging involves exchanging posts, so that both blogs get the chance at reaching a new audience. Of course, it is also possible to make a totally different arrangement. You might be willing to put some advertising on your site to direct traffic to the other blog. Or you might want to add a good review of that blog onto your own. Just as important, guest blogging will allow you to build relations with other bloggers. They might prove useful to you later on in your business's life.

Where can you find guest blogging opportunities, or advertise your own? BlogLinkedUp is a great site where to request articles for your blog, and see what articles bloggers can offer for your site. Once you sign up, you will receive an email a few times a week, providing you with potential content for your site.

Freelancers

If you are willing to pay for the content, there are many places where you can hire freelancers to research, write, re-write, or edit content for you. If you are going to employ someone, you need to make it very clear what they have to do, what level of quality you expect, what kind of measure you have in place to prevent fraud, what kind of copyright you expect. Will you licence the rights, or do you want to transfer them all to you, do you need only electronic rights, or do you want print or serial rights as well?

Looking for freelancers, the best places to go will be eLance, Freelancer.com and oDesk. You should not discount your local writers. If you leave not too far from a college or university, you may find that some students will be willing to write for you in exchange for some work experience and money. Just make sure they know what they are doing.

Distribution

Once you have created you content, you need to make sure people know it exists. Or course, most of it will end up being published on your blog. But there are other ways to distribute various formats of content.

Article Directories

We have already seen how you can use directories to source content for your site. You can of course also use them to distribute your own articles to blog owners looking for content. If you want to do this, it might be best to create articles with directories in mind. Just like any other post, these should be keyword optimised to try to get the search engine interested. You might want to include one or two pictures. These pictures could be your portrait or your blog's logo. If you are presenting or reviewing a product or service within the article, you may want to include a picture of the product.

All article directories will allow you to link back to your own blog. Some will only give you one link, others will allow more. Make sure you know how many you are allowed and use them. You can link back to a particular blog post that deal with the same content as your article. You can link back to your home page. If you are presenting/reviewing a product, you could also link to the product description or its sales page. This can be very useful for your own products, or if you are using affiliate marketing.

If you are going to distribute an article to directories, make sure you do not post it onto your blog as well. Even if you have created that content, it will be deemed duplicated content and could affect your site ranking. The best way is to create two articles: one full-length that will appear on your site; another with fewer advice that will act as a teaser onto directories.

Video Distribution

Most blogging platforms have now embraced multi-media. But if you are in need of a good software for video playback, then Flow Player might be the one for you. It also happens to be free to use in the branded version. There are many other tools that can make using video on your blog a lot easier.

The easiest way to distribute videos online remains YouTube. With your account, you can also create your own channel for other users to subscribe to. It could allow you to promote your videos – and thus your blog(s) to a wider audience. YouTube videos can easily be integrated into any websites using short pieces of code. This means that your videos could be seen by many different people if other websites decide to re-distribute them.

Re-purposing Content

This is an important concept for all bloggers to understand. Once you have created some content, you should not just let it sit on your blog. You should instead think of ways to re-use it in such a way that it will bring new or returning customers to your site.

The first thing you should realize is that most of your site's content will become old pretty quickly. Even if you were to post only once or twice a week, this would still be between twenty and forty posts written in the space of six months. Even your most loyal readers will may have missed a post or two. And your new readers may not bother looking through your archives or even searching through your site for a post that interest them.

You have to make sure to bring the content they want to them. The first step to re-purposing is to simply re-use your existing content. In the case of blogging, it means linking to your previous posts. If your theme allows – or if you have the technical know-how to hack into your theme's file – you should create category archives as well as a more general one. You should also make use of 'related posts' plugins to promote the rest of your content.

The second step is format swapping. If you have held a webinar about a particular topic, nothing stops you selling the MP3 recordings or from transcribing the recordings and using them to create an ebook. If you have written a series of posts, they could easily be transformed into a special report or a short video tutorial.

The third and final step to re-purposing is cross-platform offerings. Whatever you do on one side of your blogging business, you should make sure that your whole network knows about it. So if you have uploaded a new video to YouTube, put it on your blog as well, and let people know about it through FaceBook, Twitter, and any other social networks your blog appears on.

Checklist

To Do:

✔ Research a list of ideas for your blog.

✔ Decide which content format(s) will fit the information.

✔ Look into distribution channels for your content – other than your blog, of course.

✔ Work out how-to repurpose the content you will create or source.

3.3 Generating Revenue

As we have already seen in our introduction to blogging, the blogging business model is one where generating revenue relies entirely on your readers interactions with the sites. You will need them to click your ads, buy your affiliate products from you rather than the competition, buy your products... Here we will take a closer look at ways you can get paid through your blog.

Advertising

This is one of the most used source of income for blogs. Offering advertising space on your blog can be very useful to your readers, as they can get to know good products related to your niche. There are many ways to deploy this source of income on your own site.

You can join advertising networks to find advertising to fill your spaces. If you are looking to use them, you will need to decide on what advertising model you want to use. Most advertising programmes work with CPC or CPM.

Cost per click, or CPC, will earn you a small amount of money each times one of your readers clicks an ad on your site. This will usually not amount to much. It is probably the most used form of advertising income.

Advertising

Cost per impression, or CPM (the M stands for thousand, which is the standard number of impressions bought by advertisers), will earn you a set amount of money each time the ad is shown on your site – never mind if your reader clicks it or not.

There are many advertising programmes you can work with. The most popular remains Google Adwords. However, there are other networks you can try. AdBrite, Chikita, Link Worth, Link Share and Double Click, for example, are all good choices to fill your advertising spaces.

Alternatively, you could simply offer potential advertisers the chance to get onto your own program from your site. Managing your own advertising program can involve a lot of work. There are however ways to reduce that work load, such as using plugins or software to help you keep track of who is paying you to display what kind of advertisements, for how long. The good thing is that any money involved would be given directly to you by the advertisers, improving your cashflow. And you would not loose a share of this to whatever advertising network.

You should keep in mind that advertising can be placed on more that just your site. Google, for example, has become very good at offering such solutions. They can allow you to place ads on your RSS feeds, on your video content, and alongside search results within the site. If you are also publishing a newsletter or magazine, nothing stops you from selling advertising space within them to add another income stream to your site.

Affiliation

Affiliate marketing has really become a tool many people are using in order to earn from their blogs. Although it can take the exact same forms as advertising, the process is quite different. Where advertisers will pay you upfront for sending traffic to their sites either in the forms of clicks or impressions, affiliate marketing requires you to help close the sale. You will only receive your commission if your reader – the potential customer – goes through with buying the product you were advertising. For this to work for your blog, it requires both more targeted traffic, and more promotional efforts on your parts. However, the rewards tend to be greater than with advertising. Some very good affiliate networks – Amazon, Clickbank, CommissionJunction, Trade Doubler, Link Share and the Google Affiliate Network among them – will offer up to 80% commission for a sale. In some places, commission is a fixed price. One way or the other, commissions can easily reach $100 for one sale.

Paid-For Blogging

There are three main ways to get paid for producing blog posts. The first is to review and/or promote products and services from advertisers. Places such as PayPerPost, Sponsored Reviews and ReviewMe can put you in touch with people who are looking for bloggers to work with. You will be paid by the word or by the post. Most of these sites will only require you to write a review. You don't have to actually say that you liked the product or service, you get paid anyway, although it is best to be entirely truthful when looking to use this kind of income stream. If you constantly give bad reviews, you will soon find yourself out of work.

Another way to earn to get paid for blogging is to sign up with sites such as Suite101, HubPages, eHow and Constant Content. These will pay you either a flat fee each time that your article is read by someone, or a share of the advertising revenues your post bring in. Some of these sites expect you to own a Google AdSense account, so you can use it to get money in for the ads.

Another way to get paid for blogging is to produce content and then offer it for sale on market places such as Constant Content and TextBroker. These sites will offer both the opportunity to sale pre-written content and content written to fit an advertiser's subject and guidelines. You can also have a look on sites such as eLance, Freelancer.com and oDesk for blogging related jobs. More often than not, these will be re-writing or editing jobs. Competition can be very fierce to get hold of these jobs, and so it is up to you to build as strong a writing portfolio as you can and establish a loyal base of customers.

Your own products

Selling your own products involves a lot of work, and may not be worth the trouble if you are only hoping to earn a little from your blog. Typically, blog owners will simply promote products through affiliate marketing rather than creating their own. However, if you are looking to make a full-time income from blogging, then developing your own products will be necessary to create larger profits.

Product creation involves more work than you would think. Of course, you can do it the simplest way – just grab some PLR articles, spin them into an ebook and try to sell them on your site. But it is unlikely you will have much success this way. In order to sell enough to justify the amount of time – and often money – involved in creating your own products, you first need to make sure that there is a demand for this product. And you need to identify your potential customers. It is very likely that you will find various ideas for products during your market research for your business. Keep note of all of them. Then as you research products to promote through affiliate marketing, see if you could come up with a product that is not yet available or if you could improve a product that is already existing.

Selling Digital or Physical Products?

Digital products – such as ebooks and software – are easy to offer and deliver through any site. It is easier to sell digital products on a blog than it is to sell physical ones. Some people also do not trust smaller organizations to actually deliver the goods the first time they order from them. Digital goods are generally cheaper than their physical counterparts, and those customers with trust issues might be more willing to try out your customer services skills with a small order that is supposed to be delivered straight away. Trust comes later, after several successful transactions. You may well have to work hard to obtain it.

This however does not mean that selling physical products is impossible. For example, Amazon Associate program is a very good way to start selling physical products through affiliate marketing. You get to offer Amazon's products, offering a wide range of products to your customers without actually having to carry stocks of it. Your customers get to shop with a well-known name, who they are pretty certain will deliver the goods. Amazon gets to sell their stocks.

If and when you are willing to step it a step further, but still cannot afford to keep stocks then drop shipping may be a solution for you. You are entirely responsible for selling your chosen products, but you do not handle is the storage and distribution of said product. Your profit will come from the difference between the price you are selling the product for, and the price you pay your drop shipper for it.

Develop Services Around Your Site

There are often ways to sell services related to your blog's subject. Anything from tutoring, to mentorship programmes, to virtual assistants, and life coaches can be offered as long as it relates somehow to your subject.

Offering services can be a very large commitment in terms of your own time. It might be a good idea to make connection with freelancers and add them to your rota of potentially available workers who can take some of the load off you. You should be careful though: delivering bad services will negatively affect your blog and your business. You will quickly loose both your readers and your reputation.

Donations

Blogs – in particular blogs that just started as a hobby rather than a business – have long relied on donations to survive. There are various ways to implement this, but the simplest is to use Paypal and their donations buttons.

If you are developing your blog with a view to earn a full time income from it, this is one income source you should not rely on. People are rarely donating to blogs, because they have come to expect free information on the Internet. The current economic climate of budget cuts and recession, has also forced many people to cut down on unnecessary expenditures. Even in

Donations

good times, it is rare enough to find people willing to just donate their money to your business this way.

The best way to use donations is still to raise awareness and funds for somebody else. Nothing stops you from setting up a donation fund to benefit one of your favourite charities. You can then spread the word that your business is helping that particular charity by raising funds for them. You will not earn anything from it directly, but you will raise your business profile.

Memberships

Membership sites have been all the rage over the last few years. They allow you to create a recurring income stream, which might eliminate many cash flow problems for your business. However, keeping up with such a site is a lot more work, and you will definitely need a large amount of money to start up one of these.

In order for people to be happy paying a regular amount of money to you – however small – you will need to deliver true value for their money. When it comes to blogging, this means updating your site at least once a day, by offering great tips and how-to articles/ebooks/reports, product reviews, special offers, a very good and regular newsletter, access to product trials and exclusive products... You can also set up forums, chat rooms, or a social network, and make them available to your members only. The list could go on forever. And all of it needs to relates to your original subject.

This could mean employing one or more freelancers to help with content sourcing and development, building and maintaining relationships with advertisers and suppliers, updating and marketing your site, book-keeping and accounting, and many more little jobs. This can quickly become a full-time job, and you need to be sure you will have the capital to keep the site going for a good few months before you start making enough sales to just break even.

To Do:

✔ Research which income streams are favoured by your competitors.

✔ Work out your own income streams.

3.4 Building Relationships

The key to be truly successful in a blogging business lies with the ability to create relationships. Your visitors needs to feel like they know you, and trust you. Otherwise, they will never come back to your site, despite all your great content. The same can be told of potential advertisers and suppliers. If they feel they can't trust you, or that you won't give them your best efforts advertising their products and/or services, you will not be able to secure the discounts, special offers, or exclusive news you need to attract more people to your site. And so, you will loose potential sales.

Connecting with readers and suppliers

Creating good relationships with people – readers, advertisers, suppliers, blog owners, and everyone else you think might be able to help – is essential to building a successful blogging business. In today's world, there are many ways to get information: reading books, newspapers and magazines, watching television, listening to the radio, crawling the Internet... If you cannot connect with your readers, you will lose them to another informative media. If you do not connect with advertisers, they will spend their marketing budgets elsewhere. Suppliers will find other merchants to do business with. And with other bloggers as your friends, you may learn about the latest news in your subject after everyone else.

Your aim here should be to build trust. Few people will do business – whether it is buying a product or supplying it – with those they do not know and have come to trust somewhat. The more people get to know you, the more likely it is they will remember you when they need help or information. And if they are offered a choice between two ways to get that help, they will often choose the one they trust the most to deliver. Price is often only a secondary concern.

Engaging readers involves a lot more than creating informative content for them to read. You need to open a dialogue with them. The easiest way to do this is to ask their opinions. You could try to finish each of your posts with a question or two, asking what they thought of your post, if they know of any other related resources, or to share their point of view if it is different from yours. You can set these out in italics to attract your readers' attention to the end of the post.

Building a relationship with potential suppliers and advertisers will also involve dialogue. You need to listen to their needs, find out as much as you can about their products, then prove to them that you are more than qualified to help them distribute that product. This type of dialogue may not happen on your blog. You may have to contact them by phone, email, or even by commenting on their own blog(s). But it is worth the effort.

Optimizing Your Business for Relationships

The first thing you should keep in mind is that basic, blogging is ultimately a quite impersonal way of sharing your opinions, thoughts and advice. You will be talking at people, and will not know what they think unless they decide to engage in your conversation. Thankfully, the Internet has evolved to make relationships just a bit more personal.

Multimedia – in particular – is your friend when it comes to building relationships that will feel more personal to your readers. For example, a picture of you on your site could allow your readers to see what you look like. This very simple tip will automatically, and unconsciously, improve your relationships. People like to know who they are talking to. This needs to be used carefully though, as people are also prone to first impressions. They may not like you on sight, and refuse to change their mind. The best way is to employ a good

Optimizing Your Business for Relationships

freelancer photographer and talk with them about what you want to gain out of the picture, and how it will be used. They might be able to suggest clothes, poses, backgrounds and accessories to allow you to make a better first impression. As a general rule, the background should not be too cluttered or too distracting. You should appear relaxed and confident. Whatever you wear should not detract the attention of your readers too much from your face, but reinforce the message/image of yourself you want to put across.

The same could hold true with videos. If you can sit in front of your web cam and talk to your audience in a convincing manner, they will feel talked to rather than at. This could greatly improve your relationships with them without much effort on your part. If you are a bit shy, then practice hard in order to be comfortable before you actually post any videos. The same advice for background and clothes apply here. You want people to look at you, not be distracted by what you're wearing, or what's happening in the background. In videos, this also include background noises. If possible, you should unplug your phone and shut out everyone that could interrupt your webcast. Or find the quietest time to shoot your videos, and dedicate it to this purpose.

Communication tools are important to your business. We have already seen that comments are a good way to start a discussion with your readers. But what about when they want to engage you? You should make sure you leave as many doors open as possible for your readers and potential advertisers to get in touch with you. Email is still a tool of choice for many, and it can be easily configured to match your domain name. It makes you look more professional, and will often improve the trust factor you are looking to build. VoIP (Voice over Internet Protocol) services such as Skype can make it easy – and more important free – for people from around the world to get in touch with you. You would be surprised how many people prefer to use Skype rather than email – maybe because it is just like calling someone on the phone. In fact, Skype can easily replace your need for a dedicated business phone line.

It is important to list these on your contact page, alongside a form that will allow people to leave you a message without spamming your comment area. This should be readily available from any page on your blog. As such, it is best used as a page rather than a post, and integrated within your template rather than just linked to once in a while.

Relationship tracking will be of great importance to your business. There are many ways to keep track of the many conversations you may have going at the same time. Customer Relationship Management systems, such as SugarCRM, Dolibarr, Zoho, and Salesforce.com, can be helpful to keep track who contacts you, and when you reply to them. It may mean you have to get organised in order to enter the data into your chosen CRM system each time you interact with readers or potential advertisers or suppliers.

These tools can also soon become a great way to generate leads and ideas for good content. As your readers and others get in touch with you, they may give you some good ideas for posts, and content themes. It will be up to you to identify and take advantage of these opportunities.

More Relationships Tools

There are many ways to create the relationships you need for your blogging business to thrive. Most of them also relate to marketing, and so could appear in the next chapter as well as here...

Commenting

This is maybe the easiest way to start a discussion with people that you do not know. There are many blogs and forums on the Internet that will share your chosen topic, or at least have a few posts or forum topics that relates to it. Find those blogs and forums that are regularly visited by your target audience. The best way to start a discussion is to leave a very good comment on a post or a forum thread. It should be thought provoking, or give additional resources to the readers. Anything that will be perceived as useful will be welcome by the community.

Links – both in blog comments and in forum posts – are frowned upon nowadays and often seen as a cheap way to create backlinks. It is best to avoid using them in comments unless you know the blog owner or manager pretty well. When it comes to forums, it should be noted that

More Relationships Tools

links within posts are usually forbidden. Some still allow them in your signature file – the few lines that will appear at the bottom of each of your posts.

The easiest way to comment is to find a blog or forum that deal with your subject. Google Blog Search can be very useful here, as it will bring up only blog posts in the results. When looking for forums, you should use the advanced search to try to limit the results shown to actual forums. Find a post or thread you particularly like, disagree with, or where you can offer a different point of view or even some more information. Some people even actively encourage you to comment by asking about your particular experiences, or point of views. Then comment.

There are a few things you can do to help this relationship building exercise:

- ⏱ Keep it relevant – Remember to keep your comment relevant to the blog post or forum thread. There are enough around that with a bit of work, you can find one where your opinion will be precisely what is wanted by those reading about the subject. Going off subject just annoys bloggers and forum users.

- ⏱ Be respectful – Even if you disagree with what has been said, remember that everyone is entitled to their opinion. Not everyone will come to see your point of view either. Do not start exchanging nasty message, or your reputation will quickly start to go downhill. If someone is being particular nasty, simply report them and block them from contacting you if you can. If you do want to keep the exchange going, never post in anger. It is the quickest way to write something you will come to regret. Take a few days, then come back to the discussion.

- ⏱ Link only if necessary – Building a relationship with others does not mean pushing your content at them constantly. You need to be seen as helpful, the kind of person people can go to and not be sold at. Sure, you can add your links if it's allowed. But if you are looking to simply get people to know you, it doesn't really matter if they end up on your blog right away. Just answer their questions. Often enough, they will seek you out if they need more answers.

⏱ Be active – In order to make a name for yourself, you need to put and keep your name out there. Find the most popular blogs and forums, choose three or four you really like, and just post there. You will find that you won't have time for many more sites – in particular if you're going to include social media to your relationship building and marketing arsenals. People will get to know you on the larger sites. As they do this, their trust in you will increase as you prove yourself a helpful and knowledgeable person. More often than not, people on these more popular sites will also be members on the smaller sites, and they will pass your name around for you if you prove yourself to them.

Following others

You should be under no delusions that you will not need any help to keep your blogging business running. As with any business, the right contacts in your industry could be what makes your business a success instead of a failure.

As soon as you can identify a few people that are already are recognised experts in your chosen subject, make sure to follow them. This could be the best way to keep an eye on what is happening in your industry. Long established bloggers will have contacts and access to resources you may not have yet. Keeping track of what they post, and what they have to say, is a good way to get more content for your own site.

There are many different ways to 'follow' others. You can subscribe to their own blogs. One of the best ways to do this – in our view – is to use the Google Readers. You can follow most blogs from there, all in one place. It also has the advantage of keeping your email inbox free from multiple emails from either the blog owner or their chosen RSS feeds. One of the easiest way remains to use the social networks to keep track of what is happening with your acquaintances. The one problem with this is that you may miss an important update, or notifications about new posts of interest.

More Relationships Tools

Social Media

In our day and age, people seem to find themselves with less and less time. As such, you will need to spread your presence across a number of sites. This is where social networks and social bookmarking sites come into play. Many people now use these to keep ion touch with friends and family, as well as finding interesting articles to read across the multitude of blogs, websites, and more that populates the Internet.

Using the short posts allowed by Facebook and Twitter, you can let readers know about what is going onto your blog. You can introduce your newest the posts to your followers, and they get to choose whether they are interested enough to follow your links. Your aim should not be to get them to your site, but offer them good content, tips, and advice. They will naturally want to learn more if you have their best interests at heart.

As with blog commenting and forum posting, dealing with social media can take a lot of time away from your actual blog. It is also very addictive, and without the proper tools you might well end up spending a lot more time catching up with friends and acquaintances than you do working. There are many ways to prevent this. There are software to use such as TweetDeck and HootSuite that will allow you to manage your accounts on the major social networks. There are also a lot of modules, extensions, and plugins that will allow you to manage your accounts straight from your blog.

To Do:

✔ Make a list of people you already know in the niche you are looking to blog for.

✔ Include several ways for people to interact with you on your site: comments, contact form, email, Skype, social networks, social bookmarking sites...

✔ Be prepared to expand that list as you connect with readers, suppliers and advertisers.

✔ Look to integrate this within your ERP or CRM installation, so that all this marketing data is available in one place.

3.5 Marketing

We will now take a look at the tools you can use to market your blog. Remember that creativity is really your best asset when developing marketing your business. Use these tools as the basis for your plan, but put your own spin on them in order to customize your marketing efforts. This can also help to differentiate your offering from that of your competitors.

Search engines

In today's World Wide Web, it is near impossible to have a successful website without first making sure it is indexed by search engines. It is a simple fact that most people use search engines to find any information and websites of interest – even if they already know the web address. This has obviously been picked by even the providers of web browsing software as typing a few words in the web address bar instead of a URL will automatically launch a search engine.

Search engines have the great advantage of being generally free to use by bloggers. They thrive on information and generally make their money through other means. So getting indexed will cost you nothing. And the search engines will be happy to get your content.

Google is the search engine of choice for many Internet users. However, there are many other search engines used throughout the world and they should not be ignored. Some people also like to cross reference facts they gather from different search engines. Appearing on several of them may add to your credibility in their eyes.

Many search engines use spiders to constantly crawl the web. As long as your blog software does not block the spiders and you create links leading to your blog from other sites on the Internet, your site will eventually be found. However, you need to appear in search engine listings as quickly as possible. And so, it is better to present your site to the search engines rather than wait for them to find it.

In many cases, you can simply request a search engine to crawl your site in order for it to be ranked or updated. Given the numbers of search engines though and the fact that your blog needs updating each time you post something new on it, submitting your site could become a full time job. Alternatively, there are programmes designed to make this job faster. Search engine submitters can easily be found on the Internet and will do the job of submitting your site for you. Some are pretty light weight and can easily be run in the background of your PC while you work on creating posts or marketing your site. You can run these as often as needed in order to keep the search engines up to date with your content.

Google likes to make things very easy. You can submit your URL to the search engine by using the Webmaster Tools. They also have the more specific Google Blog Search. You can their pinging service to update their record as often as you publish a new post.

> **PING-O-MATIC**
>
> This nice little website could save you a lot of time overall. Ping-O-Matic allows you to ping some of the best blog services available and have them update their database with your new content. And it is as easy and simple as filling a form and ticking a few boxes.
>
> Ping-O-Matic was created by the WordPress Foundation – the same people behind the free and popular WordPress blogging platform. Following their philosophy of "serving the public good through freely accessible software," Ping-O-Matic is absolutely free to use.

Search Engine Optimisation

SEO is a very important tool in search engine marketing. Research has shown that most Internet users never make it past the first page of search results. And even less make it past page five. This is in part due to the fact that results past the first few pages often are less relevant to the particular search. But people also are impatient and often happy with the first answer they get. SEO can allow you to get placed in search results higher in search results than your competitors and so be found more often than they are.

Search engines all use keywords in order to find the most relevant content for their users. A s a blogger, it is up to you to make sure you choose the most relevant keywords for your article and then place them into your blog for best effect. Although all search engines have slightly different ways to judge your use of keywords, there are ways to get better rankings that work for most of them.

🕒 Meta Content

This is the content your users can't see, but the search engines look at first. Meta content contains title, keywords, and description. All these should use the keywords you have identified for your particular post. This will allow the search engines to know what your post is about without looking at it.

🕒 Post Content

Your actual post should also be keyword-rich in order to achieve better ranking. Things like putting the main keyword in the post title, repeating it in the post, and apply styling such as bold, italics and underline to these keywords will all allow better ranking. However, do not go overboard with these or you might get penalised.

🕒 Sitemaps

Search engines like these as they allow them to crawl though a site a lot quicker. The feature was developed with static pages in mind – that is pages you find in 'normal' websites. However, it can be adapted for blogs easily enough. Use static pages to develop an archive – with links to all your former posts. You can even do the same with your categories.

🕒 Links

Most search engines love links, in particular if they lead from somewhere on the Internet to your blog. This is why link building – the practice of creating these links leading to your site – is just as important as keywords use. Bear in mind that only permanent links are truly useful in link building. For example, advertising online will create a link back to your site. But this link will disappear s soon as your advertising campaign ends. If you concentrate on building permanent links – links that will not disappearing unless purposefully taken off – you will find that your SEO efforts will be far more rewarding.

Remember that SEO is a continuous effort. You will need to keep your list of keywords up to date, and research new ones as and when necessary for a particular post. You should update your sitemap as often as necessary to ensure your site can be crawled efficiently by the search engines' spiders.

Link Building

As we have just seen, link building is part of your SEO efforts. Internet marketers will often say how important it is for a website in terms of getting a better rank. However, link building is also a public relation tool as it can allow you to communicate with past and potential customers outside of your blog. Each link, as well as being a route to access the content to your site, is a way to put your name out there. Even if Internet users do not click immediately on your name, they might do once they have seen it on a few different websites. There are many ways to create backlinks to your site.

Your email signature

As a start up business, you may not have customers yet. But you do have contacts. And any of them could be interested in what you have to say. This is why your link building efforts should start with your email. An email signature is generally easy to set up. It can automatically be added to the end of each of the emails you send.

Signature are usually short and to the point. They may just consist of your own name and that of your blog, along with a link. Some add a slogan or catch phrase in order to get people to remember them better. If you have set up your email programme to send in HTML, then the reader will just have to click your link to be sent to your site. Even if you can't send in HTML, or your reader prefer to receive emails in text format, most people are now used to copy/pasting. They will still be able to visit you as long as you have spelled your site address right.

Once you have set up this feature, make sure to use it as often as possible. Use your email signature when you contact potential suppliers and freelancers. This is also the place to add more contact details, such as Skype ID, phone numbers and alternative email addresses. Your business contacts may well be grateful for the ability to get back to your site easily. Friends and family can be very useful as a small way to network. They may know of people in need of information you can provide through your blog. But if they don't know about your blog, they cannot help. Finally, your blog readers need to be reminded that you exist from time to time. Remember that the more people know about your site, the more chances there are that they – or someone they know – might have an interest in what you're doing.

Blog Comments

We have already looked at commenting from the perspective of building a relationship with your readers and suppliers. Commenting is also a very good marketing tool. It is a useful way to both create backlinks and increase your reputation – as long as it is done properly. Most blogs will have a set of rules, letting you know what can and cannot be included in your comment. Some bloggers do not look kindly on linking within the actual comment because it takes their readers away. If in doubt, ask. Or you could build the worst kind of reputation for yourself.

When commenting with marketing in mind rather than building a relationship, you should define what action you require of the readers, if any. You may simply want a backlink, your name put out there, or actual visitors to your site. Your comment should be written carefully with this goal in mind. Your backlink will be easily achieved, whatever your comment says, as long as your comment is approved. If your looking for exposure, simply write your blog's name in the comment somehow. This – along with your other promotional efforts – will increase the likelihood of potential customers remembering you when needed. If you really want visitors, consider adding a link within the post – if allowed – or giving enough information about your blog that the readers can easily find you.

The popularity of the blog you have chosen to comment on can only help yours. The more that blog is read, the more likely it is that people will click through to your own. However, you should not judge a blog by its comment. Many blogs have few comments, but many readers. The best ways to determine popularity is to ask the webmaster or owner for traffic statistics. However, do not ignore small blogs either. You never know when you may make a very useful connection.

If you think you can pull it off, you could target simply your market rather than your subject. If your blog is about cycling, nothing stops you from targeting a holiday-related blog with either a comment or a guest blog post about cycling holidays. But these comments and posts are the ones that have to be carefully thought out before you implement them. They could easily backfire...

do-follow and no-follow?

If you have tried to learn a bit more about links before, you may know there are to sorts of backlinks: do-follow and no-follow. The difference between them lies in how they are treated by search engines. Do-follow links will be crawled by spiders and direct them to your site to crawl it in turn. These links will count towards your SEO efforts, and hopefully improve your rankings.

No-follow links will not be crawled, and thus not be considered as a backlink by search engines. Many Internet marketers will tell you not to bother with these links and to make sure that the sites and blogs you comment on all allow the spiders to crawl back to your own site.

We take a different view to this problem. Both links are useful, but for slightly different reasons. If you are looking to boost your SEO performance, then it is right you should concentrate on finding and using do-follow links. If in doubt, simply contact the webmaster of the site you are looking to comment on and ask. Most will be happy to help in hope you become a regular reader.

Link Building

However, no-follow links can be just as useful as do-follow if you are looking to boost your reputation more than your SEO. The more insightful and useful comments and post you leave on relevant blogs and forums, the more your reputation will grow. Within a few months or years, you could be known as an expert in your field and people will know your name and that of your blog.

Forum Posting

Forum posting has long been another traditional way to promote a blog. It is simple enough to find a forum dealing with your chosen niche. The most challenging part is to become an active user and to stay active once you have started to use a few forums.

Just as their little brothers the blogs, forums are interactive. They allow for direct communication between you and your potential readers and customers. They also allow for the spread of word-of-mouth. As such, they should be treated very carefully.

Forums are generally divided into threads or topics. When posting, you should make sure to keep to the initial subject of the discussion. Anything else will annoy users greatly, and may even be treated as spam by the moderators. Well crafted posts answering the initial question will earn you the respect of other users. The best way to make a name for yourself in a forum is to be particularly helpful. Answer the queries of other users. Offer help and advice. Being polite, and writing clearly will also be good for your image.

Forums can also be used to build your publicity efforts. If you have answered a question in a particular post and you can link to it, perfect! If you can't, use your blog's full name when mentioning it, and name that post as well as the tags and categories it appears under. The more people see your name, the more they will remember it. And the more people will be directed to you by friends who knew about your blog without having visited it once.

It should be noted that forums used to welcome links. Many do not any more because of abuse and spam. As such, you should always read the rules carefully before posting any sort of link within your post – including inside your signature. As well as a link building, forums should now be regarded as a communication and publicity tool.

Directories

Just as we have phone books offline, we have directories online. These are quite simply databases – some of them very large – allowing people to find a particular website/business/subject of interest without having to crawl through endless Google results. From an SEO point of view, they are also a cheap and easy way to collect backlinks.

Directories are usually quite specific in the data they gather. Some are nothing more than business directories, offering simple contact details and a link back to a main website if the company has one. Website directories do the same thing for this type of data.

The best two directories for a blogging entrepreneur are blog and RSS feeds directories. Blog directories will direct to you potential readers who are looking for up to date content about a particular subject. RSS feeds directories can go a step further by showing the latest posts on various blogs that deal with a subject.

You should try to get listed by as many directories as possible. As well as boosting your SEO efforts, they will also allow you a small but highly targeted influx of traffic.

Article Marketing

Article marketing is another way to bring traffic to your blog. Many bloggers use article directories to provide their own sites and blogs with ready-made content. In return for you writing that content, you get to put a link to your blog or site in the last paragraph of the article – also known as the bio box. A bio box generally consists of a few sentences, presenting yourself and your blog, website, business and/or product. You can also link back to your site.

Although the agreement of most article directories says that website owners should reproduce the articles word for word, many do not do this any more. Many search engines – Google primary among these – have started to penalize sites with too much duplicated content. These sites have seen their ranks fall sharply over the past twelve to twenty-four months. As such, many are now using article spinners and rewriters to change the wording of articles. Many even go as far as removing the bio box.

Article Marketing

This is not to say that article marketing is now a thing of the past. But just as forum posting, it should now be used as a promotional tool as well as an SEO one. You need to put your actual blog's name into the copy of your article. There is less chance of unscrupulous writers blotting out your name this way.

Email Marketing

This tool is essential if you intend to use direct selling on your blog. In order to contact potential buyers, you first need to know who they are and how to contact. Your email list will provide you with this information, and more if your think it through properly.

List Building

As a small start-up, one of your priorities should be to build your email list in order to have access to as large as possible a number of potential customers. List building is not necessarily difficult, but it can be time consuming. There are a few ways to do this as quickly as possible.

- Landing Pages

Research has shown that the use of landing pages in conjunction with email marketing increase the rate of conversion.

Landing pages are simple in design. They also require one single action from your potential readers. Because of the uncluttered feeling of these pages, Internet users are not distracted by other information and can concentrate on what you want them to do. The only links found on these pages are usually found in the footer and link to the privacy policy, the terms and conditions, and the main site. Those running affiliate programmes often put a link there to allow affiliate marketeer to take part.

Before creating your landing page, you should identify what it is you want your visitors to do: sign up for your newsletter, buy a product, become a member... Your landing page should be designed so that it is the only thing your visitor can do on that page. You can redirect them to your actual site after you have gotten them to do what you want.

⏱ Free Products

Many people cannot resist being given something. It always feel like they are receiving a bargain. Offering a free product of some kind in exchange for subscribing to your newsletter usually works well. The rest of your offerings have to be worth it though, or your new subscribers will leave just as soon as they have receive the free product from you.

⏱ Special Offers and Discounts

In the same vein as the above, offering a time-limited offer or discount can help to build your list. Using sales promotion tactics will only truly work if you have control over the final retail price of a product, or if you have negotiated a deal with the manufacturer and/or distributors of that product. Your potential readers will once again feel like they are getting additional value in exchange for their contact details. This may be all they need from you, but it could also turn them in regular readers.

⏱ Safelists

Safelists are groups of Internet users who have agreed to receive promotional emails from other members of the group. In exchange, they also get the chance to sent such emails without being marked as a spammer.

These are potentially huge amounts of people willing to receive mails from other members of the safelist. Although some lists are small, it is not unusual to find some with more than 10,000 members ready to view your site.

The conversion rates of this method are not always great. Many users simply click to get the points required to send their own promotional mails. However, you may find that some of the lists are exceptionally responsive to some offers. Given it is possible to new customers for no financial outlay, safelists should not be entirely discarded from your marketing tool kit

⏱ Buy or Rent a List

This method should be used with the utmost care. They are many places on the Internet where you can find email lists to buy or rent. Always check that the business selling you those lists has done their job properly. Users should know they are on the lists, and should be happy to be contacted.

Spam has become an international problem, and laws have been put in place around the world to combat it. Make sure you do not fall victim to unscrupulous dealers selling you stolen email addresses. Only deal with those who can present you with proof that their lists were acquired legally.

> **TIP: List as a research tool**
>
> Do not fall into the trap of never researching through your list, and only selling to it. Your market research efforts should be continuous in order to identify new markets and develop new products.

List Handling

Once you have gathered a number of email addresses, you need to make the best use of them possible. It is important to remember that your list will only responsive if you customize your messages to your subscribers. Trying to sell something your subscribers have no interest in will result in them removing their email address from your list.

There has also been controversy about the frequency you should send messages. Many Internet marketers think it is essential to keep in daily contact with their lists. Some even post to their members several times a day. However, you need to remember that your readers will be contacted by you in many different ways – through Twitter and Facebook for examples. You will need to work out how much is too much contact for your particular niche and readers.

There are several companies that can help you to take care of your list automatically. MailChimp, GetResponse and Aweber are probably the most used services. Each will allow you to gather emails from your site and have them directly added to their respective database. It will also allow you to comply with the law by making it easy for your readers to unsubscribe if they decide to. These services allow you add an automatic unsubscribe link to the emails they sent your subscribers.

Remember that with email marketing, you will fall under both the Data Protection and the anti-spam legislations. You need to develop a privacy policy explaining to your readers how their details are handled by you, what you will and will not do with it, and how they can get in touch to modify whatever data you hold about them.

Advertising

Advertising remains the most used marketing tool, both on- and offline. Since you are launching an Internet business, it is evident that you will think first and foremost of online advertising. And this will most probably be the best was to spend your advertising budget. But you should not forget about offline advertising altogether.

There are various way to buy advertising online. Pay-Per-Click is probably the most well known thanks to Google and their AdWords programme. PPC is particularly efficient if you are looking to get qualified visitors to your blog – that is readers that really want to know about a particular subject or product you are blogging about.

CPM is a variant of the above and means cost per thousand impressions. This way of advertising is better if you are looking for exposure more than actual readers. This may sound strange – why would you be looking for people to know about you, but not for them to follow through to your site. However, you should remember that the more people hear about you, the greater the chances of them remembering and buying from you when they need your kind of services.

CPA – or cost per action – has become widespread thanks to affiliate marketing. We will look into this form of marketing in more details later. CPA is a performance-based advertising model. In affiliate marketing, it means paying a commission to the sales agent as and when they close a sale for you. However, the original CPA model does not necessary involve a sale. The action required could be anything from bringing unique visitors to your site, to getting people to enquire about a particular product or service, or registering to receive marketing messages. The action could be anything you need. The advantage of this model is that you can use it to increase more than simple sales. It can be very useful to build your email marketing list.

Advertising

There are many big players in online advertising, and it can't hurt to learn a bit about them. Of course, Google and their AdWords programme are probably well known by most. This programme has two real advantages:

1. Your ad will only be shown to people who are interested in your subject, product, or services. In other words, you will receive targeted traffic to your site and thus have a greater chance to secure a sale.

2. You have a chance at stealing customers away from your competitors. Although bidding on your competitors is highly frowned upon – not to mention illegal in many cases – you can still use the same keywords. Your ad will then have a chance to appear alongside search results, even if someone is looking for your competitors by name. A well-written ad and a good special offer could easily sway potential readers to you.

Other programmes using pay-per-click are BidVertiser, Microsoft adCenter, and Yahoo! Search Marketing. There are also bid management programmes that can help to manage all your PPC advertising bids from one place. If you have several campaigns running with different advertising programmes, you can try Atlas One Point or BidRank. Facebook is also a very good place to advertise. It can offer both CPC and CPM. If you really would prefer CPM to CPC, then you can try programmes such as Advertising.com, Adtegrity, and Clicksor.

Offline advertising can also be very useful to your blog, as long as you target your market very carefully. During your research, you will have come across specialist magazines dealing with your chosen niche. These are the publications you should target when looking to advertise offline. They are advantageous for two reasons:

1. They are generally cheaper to advertise in than broader publications, such as newspapers.

2. They are already targeted towards your own markets.

If you can match the writing style of the magazine, you might also want to pay for advertising features – a cross between a press release and an advertisement, generally featuring both an article and a display ad presenting your business/blog/product/service to potential customers.

Not all publication allow them, but it is always good to enquire. An advertising feature can also allow you to target slightly different markets if necessary. For example, your local paper might not be able to print a simple press release for you – because a small publication is always in need of money – but they might be amenable to an advertising feature.

However you decide to advertise, remember to put processes in place to track the results of your efforts. Programmes such as Google AdWords pride themselves in making it all very easy. You should definitely take advantage of this is you can. Track your bids, find out which keywords work better than others, find out if worded ads work better than display and why, track your visitors while they are on your site as well – do they visit your home page and leave, or do they look around?

If you are advertising offline, make use of codes to track where your visitors hear about you. It can be useful to use of discounts with these codes so your visitors have a good incentive to give you these codes. You get better information about how they find you, and they will probably be happy about the savings.

Public Relations

The advent of the Internet – and in more recent years, that of social media and social marketing – has made public relations a lot easier to handle for many small business owners.

As well as relying on traditional media to promote your business, you can now contact and keep in touch with your potential, current and past customers for very little financial outlay.

> **TIP: Press release and SEO**
>
> Once your press release is available on the web, it can – and will – be found by the search engines. As such you should be sure to use your main keywords in your release. Also, remember to include a link to your site in the last paragraph. This will help your site's ranking a little bit.

Press Release

This remains the main tool of PR. Writing a good press release will allow journalists to know precisely whether the news is of interest to their publication(s), what to write in their own articles, and whom to contact for more information if necessary. Generally, a press release will be no more than one sheet of paper. Title and sub-title are printed in much larger font than the rest of the release, and written to grab the reader's attention. The first paragraph will usually the basic questions of WHO, WHAT, WHEN, WHERE, and WHY. The second paragraph will develop on the first and the third will generally contain a long quote from a relevant person. The last paragraph will give the journalist the contact details of the person in charge, in case they would like to feature a longer interview or article and need more information.

Once you have written your release, you should distribute as widely as possible. The Internet can make that pretty easy. Many sites offer press release distribution, whether free or for a fee. Prweb.com, PRLeap.com, ClickPress.com, and PRLog.org are but just a few. During market research, you may also have identified particular blogs, websites, e-zines, magazines, newspapers, radios, and TV shows that your readers use to get information. These are the media you should target with your press releases. Don't expect them to go looking for your releases. Contact them ahead of time and ask for a named contact to send your release to. This could be an editor, webmaster, or simple journalist. Send them the release then a week or so later, contact them to make sure they have received it. The other place to put your release on is your website. It will allow journalists to quickly and easily learn more information about you and your blog. The best Place to put this is in your online media kit.

Social Networks

They have the great advantage to put you in direct contact with many more potential readers. They also are a very good public relation tool as they allow you to keep an eye on what people think of you and your products. It is almost impossible to control what people say about you and your products – whether on or offline. But through social networks, you will have the opportunity to address whatever worry potential readers/customers may have. This can only give you a good reputation when it comes to customer service.

Once you have started to market your blog through the social networks, you can find that it takes hours to keep updating each and every site every other day or so. And this is what is needed to keep your readers interested and coming back to your blog.

Networking tools such as HootSuite, MarketMeSuite, Awareness and MediaFunnel are precisely what you need to cut down on the amount of time you spend social marketing. They will allow you to access and post to your social media from one place. This could give you much more time to concentrate on developing new content.

Checklist

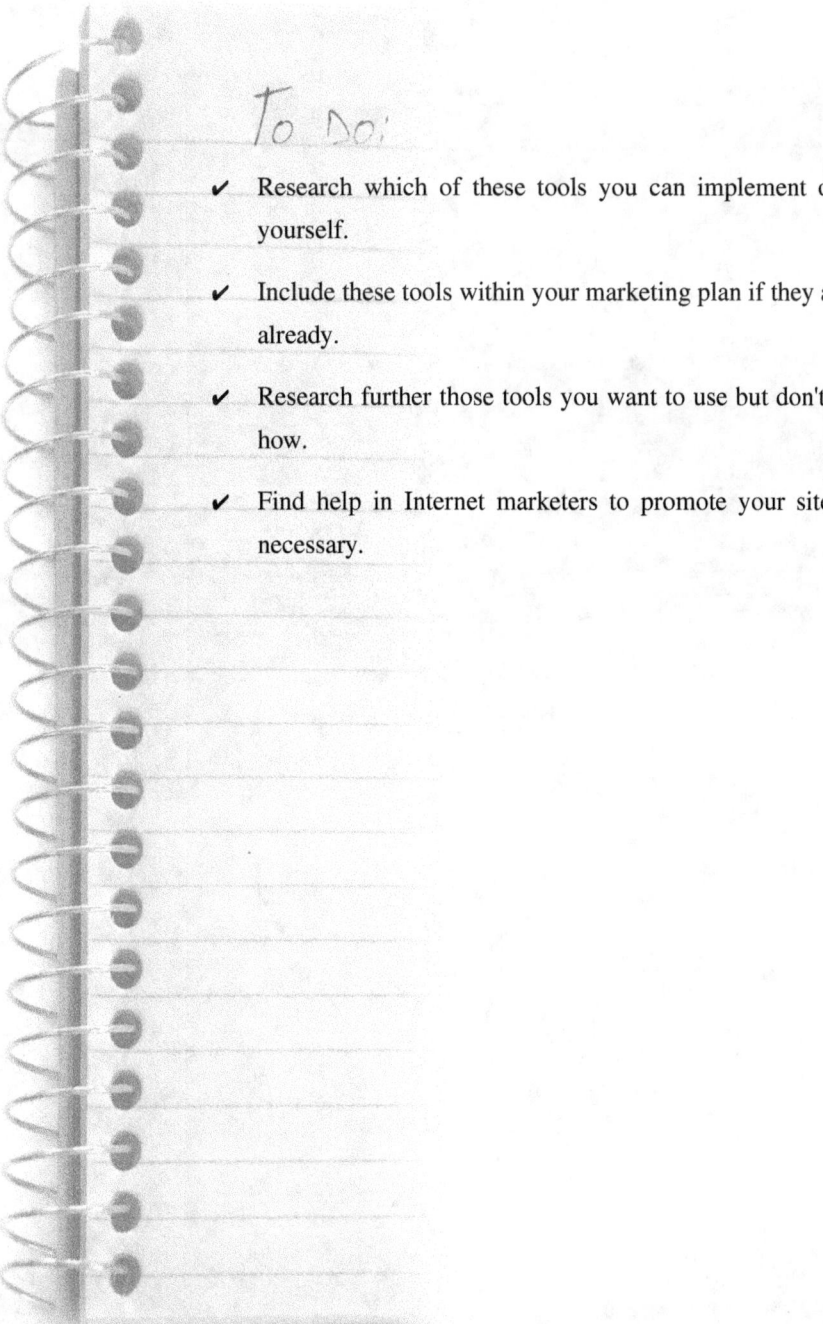

To Do:

✔ Research which of these tools you can implement on your site yourself.

✔ Include these tools within your marketing plan if they are not there already.

✔ Research further those tools you want to use but don't know quite how.

✔ Find help in Internet marketers to promote your site for you if necessary.

4 – Expanding

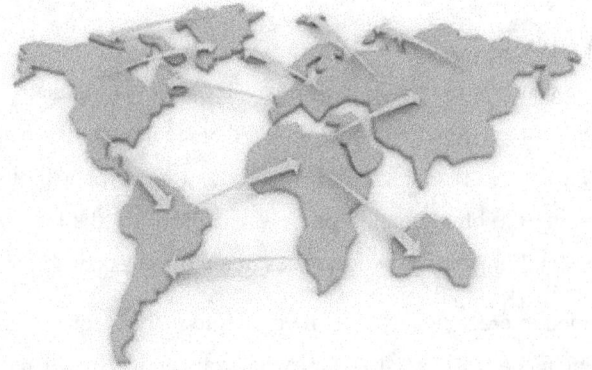

4.1 Grow your business

Once your business is established, you should decide what you want to do with it. Stagnation is not a good thing for any business. Your readers may come back to your blog when they need information about your subject, but this need will change overtime to other subjects, related or not. It is up to you to make sure your business keeps up with these changes.

Creating a Blog Network

Once you have create you first blog, nothing stops you from creating many more blogs. There are ways to automate so many functions of blogging that creating a blog from scratch can take you less than thirty minutes. If you are only looking to blog for a living, then creating a network and automating the blog creation precesses is probably the best option for you and your business. Then simply repeat the processes as many times as needed to create your blogs.

Once you have decided to create a network, there is little reasons for you to keep to the same target markets and/or niche subjects. The aim with your network will be to reach as many people as possible across a wide variety of subject in order to maximize your profits.

Creating a Blog Network

You should also keep an eye on the fashionable subjects to blog about. People often tend to be taken in by the latest trends. You have to be able to capitalize on this as and when it happens. This is where constant market research comes in. You need to identify those markets as they appear, because they do not stick around for very long.

Keyword research is vital here, and it might actually be a good idea to employ a market researcher – or an SEO expert with a good deal of experience – so they can help you to discover these niche markets as they grow. Most of these fad niches come and go very quickly, so you

> **TIP:Hosting**
>
> If you are going to create a network, don't skimp on hosting. You will need a very reliable hosting provider to constantly deliver your blogs. Hostgator is one of the best providers around. They also offer unlimited domain add-ons, which can be very useful for a blog network.

need to be able to discover these markets, create your blog and promote it in record time.

The key to this will be automation. There are software available that will allow you to automate many processes of blogging – such as blog set up, content creation, and traffic generation. If you manage this, you will be well on your way to creating a blog network.

Finding New Niches

We have already taken a long look at researching niches to blog about in part two of this book. Finding new niches for you to blog about is just a matter of repeating the process.

Related niches

There is something to be said to keeping to a closely related subject when thinking about creating a new blog to expand your business with. If your new niche is related in some manner to that of your original blog, you may save yourself a lot of work. It is very likely that your current readers will also be interested in your new niche. And thus, you should be able to simply promote your new blog to your current readers, exchange links between the two sites, and quickly get your new blog up and running.

The other good thing about related subjects is that you will have built yourself a reputation in your first chosen subject. Since you are now talking about a closely related subject, you can carry on to build your reputation in the same sector. You can even use your reputation as a boost to promote your new blog. If potential customers ask around about you, there is a good chance that other users will recommend you, your sites and your products just because you already have a good reputation in your field.

Finding related niches is quite easy. Just look at your posts. You may have covered several closely related niches in some way already. This is another way to re-purpose content. If you have not yet covered related niches in your first blog, you simply need to do some research. This is where keywords tools can be useful once more. Simply type in your current keywords, and see what else is being searched for.

New interests, same readers
We have pointed out before that market research should be something you do all the time. If you have followed our advice, you should have access to a wealth of information about your current readers. If not, now can be the time for you to find out more about them. If you were to learn about their other interests, you could create your next blog to cater to them.

A simple way to learn more about your readers is to organize surveys. Ask them what they are interested in – apart from the subject you are dealing with in your current blog. With the answers, you will have a long list of potential subjects to blog about. For example, if your first blog was about gaming and targeted at fifteen to twenty-four years old, you may find that they are also interested in music, movies, or maybe popular TV shows.

Then it is up to you to research your new niche, and create appealing content. You will have the advantage of already knowing your readers, so you can customize your writing style to appeal to them. You will also have a ready-made audience to promote your new blog to – either post a quick intro or review on your current blog, or simply by advertising there.

Optimizing Your Readership

If you think your blog can gain more readers, you can try to find new markets interested in your niche. First of all, you should go back to your original research and make sure that you identified the right primary market. It could be that you have made a simple mistake there and have focused your marketing efforts on a secondary market rather than the primary.

If you are looking to expand your readership, have a look at your research and try to identify secondary markets to target. If you are sure that your primary market is right, secondary markets will be easy enough to find. They will relate to your primary markets in two to three major ways. As we have already noted, all your readers will be Internet users. And they will all have an interest in your chosen subject. However, they may vary in age group, location, income and education levels, and other interests may differ slightly. Your job is to find out which of these attributes to target for better results.

Finding Staff

If you have started to make plans for expansion, you need to decide whether you can carry on by yourself or if you need to bring in outside help. The first step would be to establish what you would like to remain in complete control of and which tasks you are willing to delegate. Second, is deciding how many people will need to be brought in to do the job. But before all that, you need to make sure you know what is involved in employing someone.

Employment laws and regulations

There are a whole lot of rules that come with employing someone. For example, you will need to pay your staff at least the Minimum Wage. This changes every year so you need to keep an eye out for it. You would also be responsible for collection National Insurance and Income Tax out of your employees' wages to then hand it over to Revenues & Customs. This can be worked around if your freelancers are self employed – and thus responsible for paying their own taxes. If your freelancers also happen to be foreign nationals, it is best to contact you local Business Link and/or tax office to find out about taxes and employment regulations in this particular case. If you employ more than five people, and all work from an office, you would also fall under the Health & Safety regulations. For example, you would need to have a first aid kit, a designated and somewhat trained first aid person, a planned route to exit the building in case of a large fire, and a fire extinguisher.

Defining what and who

Explain exactly what your employee will be expected to do. Will they be required to write posts? Will they need to do the research for them as well? Will they simply re-write content to your specification? Will they be expected to create other types of content – such as video, audio, Tweets, Facebook messages? If you are looking for a marketeer, do you want someone who will handle both offline and online marketing? Will they be required to take on some market research as well? Will they need to develop your marketing plan, or simply help to implement the plan you have already created?

Define how much you are willing to pay. Will you pay on a commission basis, per job, or per hour? Will there be a sliding scale based on performance? Will the job be full or part-time? Will the staff be employed or freelance? Can you offer any benefits? Will your staff work from home or from an office? Answering these question will create your job description and put you in mind of the kind of person you are looking for.

Once you know what you want your staff to do, define who they have to be to fit in your business. Decide what qualities and qualifications you are looking for. In a blogging business, they should at least be good with computers and the Internet, in particular if they will be responsible for updating the site or market it. If they are going to be responsible for creating content, researching and writing skills are a must. If they are teleworking for you from across the world, you need to be able to contact them easily – access to Skype, a chat service, and/or email might be a must.

Job boards

Once you have refined your ad, you need to put it out there. The first step is to contact your local Job Centre. They will be able to put your job listing on their databases. There are also loads of place online where you can put your ad. Craiglist can also be a good place to

Finding Staff

advertise any vacancies you have. If you're looking for freelancers to help you, then sites such as Freelancer.com, eLance, and oDesk can be very useful. A large number of freelancers are always looking for work there, and some have been around long enough to have build quite a good reputation.

4.2 Develop new products and services

Once you have decided to expand your blogging business, you have to think further than your blog. You have to remember that your first blog – although you might feel very attached to it – is only a product. There many other products and services you can set up to compliment that first offering. Or diversify your markets.

Product Creation

We have already looked into product creation as a potential source of income for your blog. If you have not already implemented this technique to generate profits for your blog, now is the time to do it.

Research

Anything can be sold online. The real problem for you is to find out which type of products your readers will really be interested in. Market research comes in again here. Only now that you have some subscribers, you can gather primary data by asking your readers to answer a few questions.

Blog

Product Creation

SurveyMonkey and Kwik Survey are two online survey tools you can use to create your surveys. You may also be able to find a plugin or add-on for your particular blogging platform that will allow you to conduct surveys and polls straight from your blog. Of course, you should ask them what they would like to see on the blog, and what kind of products they want to buy. But you should also get to know them better. Find out who they are, their interests, their goals in life... The more you learn about them the easier it will be for you to create products they will want to buy from you.

Product Development

Once you have done your research, you can start planning your products. The advance of the Internet and printing technologies has made it possible for small businesses to offer the same kind of products large companies can. Digital products – such as ebooks and software – have been very popular with both Internet users and businesses because they allow customers to access the product straight after paying for it. No need to wait for delivery.

However, the advances in print technologies – particularly those of digital printing and print-on-demand – have made it possible for small businesses to compete with the larger companies. Entrepreneurs can now publish books and magazines, create mugs, calendars, t-shirts, cds, dvds, and many other products without the upfront costs of ordering large numbers and warehousing.

Once you have created your new products, you can sell them on your site. You can use them to simply bring in more readers by promoting your new product as widely as you do your blog.

Buying and Selling Blogs for Profits

In business, many successful people are not such much entrepreneurs as they are investors. They put money into a business with the sole aim to sell it – or whatever share they own – at a large profit. The equivalent also existing in the blogging industry. It is generally known as web flipping.

Getting the blogs

If you decide to go down this route, you will need several blogs. You need to keep in mind that people buying blogs do so because they want a ready-made business. Preferably one that is guaranteed to make them some money. They will also expect a design to match their chosen niche, and some content pre-loaded into the site.

There are two ways to get a blog matching these expectations. The first is to build it from scratch. In the simplest terms, you design and develop a site for a particular niche, and upload some content on it. You will then need to repackage the site to make it as easy as possible for the new owner to set up the site. This is usually best achieved by modifying the source files to include template and content. These kinds of ready-made site are often also called turnkey sites.

Second is to buy a ready-made site, and develop it to the point where you can sell it on for a profit. The simplest is to find a site with a proven audience, a decent number of subscribers, and that is already generating a profit for its current owner. From there, your job will be to increase these factors in order to resell the site for more than what you have paid and invested into it. Slightly harder in terms of the work involved is to buy a turnkey site and work to make it take off.

Selling on

When deciding to go into web flipping, you should carefully define what your exit strategy will be. That is, the point at which you think it reasonable to sell the business on rather than carry on with it. Planning your exit, you should take into consideration three scenarios:

- if your blog grows more or less as you expected

- if your blog becomes hugely successful

- if your blog fails altogether

Under each scenario, you need to decide under which circumstances you will sell, your asking price, and how low you are willing to go.

Buying and Selling Blogs for Profits

Obviously, the site itself will partly define the price. Turnkey sites are usually sold at quite low prices. This is because the template is not unique, the content given away is generally PLR, and the site is not live – giving absolutely no guarantees to the buyer that they will see a return on their investment.

Selling a site that is live – by opposition – will attract a higher price. However, this will be entirely dependent on daily and monthly traffic, size and health of the email list, and current profits. It is entirely possible that potential buyers will ask to see proofs of any claims you make about the facts above. Consequently, it may be a good idea to have these ready. Also keep in mind that some people do not trust easily. They may not believe the first proof you present them. Have screen shots and videos of your affiliate and traffic analysis accounts ready to show them. Maybe even contact some regular users to act as references.

Blogging for Other Businesses

You could try to promote your services to other businesses. Many businesses – local and small businesses in particular – are interested in developing their own blog, but do not have the time and/or expertise to do so.

You could promote yourself as a blogger for hire, offering to blog about their businesses for a fee. It can be a good idea to play on your real strengths and likes here. If your strengths are planning, designing and developing blogs, then you can offer these services under a 'web design' header. If you prefer to research and write blog posts and/or social media messages, then nothing stops you from approaching businesses with an offering of managing their blogs and social networks for them.

Whether the business in question already has a blog designed, or needs one done from scratch, is near enough irrelevant – unless you manage to close that designing-and-developing deal for your business. The point here is to offer small and local businesses with a chance to participate in the social revolution that blogging has become, without having to commit their own time to do it.

4.2 Develop new products and services

The key to success would be to work out exactly how much your clients would be willing to pay for this service. Too high a price point would defeat your purpose, too low and you would quickly make too much of a loss to carry on offering the services. You will also need very good business connections

4.3 Funding Growth

Finding the funds to expand your business can be just as difficult as finding enough to start up. The same possibilities will be opened to you. But a lot more will be demanded from you and your business.

The Plans

Just as when you looked to start your business, you will need to justify to any potential investors how you plan to spend the sudden influx of funds. Once again, your business and marketing plans will make the difference between you securing that money or not.

More often than not, investors will expect more detailed plans when expanding than when starting up. After all, you will have been in your business for a little while now, and you will be expected to know a lot more about what you can and cannot do, how your industry is faring, and the best ways to market both your blogs and your business. It is impossible to tell you precisely what people will be looking for when thinking about investing further into your business. Obviously, they will want to make sure your ideas for growth are sustainable. They will want to be sure you will be able to repay the money as and when they ask.

Your business plan will need to do more than just map out what you intend to do over the next couple of years or so. You will need to explain what you have done over the years you have been in business to get in this position. You will also need to explain what you intend to do in the future, both near and further away. After a year or so in business, investors will expect you to have worked out both short and long terms goals for your business, and this should be reflected in your business plan. This could mean launching new blogs, creating products, striking new deals with suppliers or advertisers, offering new services...

Your marketing plan should demonstrate how you plan to spend the increased marketing budget you will have. An increase in size will generally mean the need to increase your readership and sales in order to sustain the pressure put on your business by the new loan repayments. It is very important to plan how you will bring about this increase in revenues. If you don't plan to launch any new product or service, you will need to rely entirely on your marketing to bring more people to your site(s) in order to get more sales.

The Potential Investors

As we have seen when looking at starting up your business, there are many ways to invest in a business. The same hold true when you are looking to expand that business, and the same ways to find funds are available.

Your Own Funds

This is the most logical way to raise money. Simply re-invest your profits into the business. Of course, this is not always the best option. It can also be difficult in times of economic trouble. But it is still the best way to raise funds for growth, because you do not take on any debt. As when you were looking to start up, it is unlikely that anyone will be willing to help if you are not prepared to put at least some of the money needed forward.

It is important that you take stock of your position well before you decide to develop a strategy for growth, and assess how much would be needed to take your business to the level you desire it to be at. You will then need to see how much of this amount you can afford to re-invest. The difference will be what you need from outside investors.

Banks

These should be your first port of call. You should go carefully through any agreement you have with your current bank and determine with your bank manager if further lines of credit could be extended to your business. Now is the time to ask about overdraft, credit cards, leasing agreements, hire purchases, and what else they might be able to offer you. Anything that might help you to easy your cashflow.

Getting a second business loan is very unlikely, unless you have very solid business and marketing plans. However, if you have finished repaying the first one and had no problems with late payments or arrears, your bank might well consider you a safe bet for further lending. Again, your planning needs to be spotless.

A NOTE ON FRIENDS AND FAMILY

Although your friends and family might well be your first port of call if you need to borrow money to start your business, they might not be able to help here. Even if a blogging business can be relatively cheap to run, growing a business usually is considerably more expensive as you will be planning for the long term. As such, you will probably be asking for more money than before. Your friends and family might well want to help, but they should be aware of the risks, and of the fact that their money will be tied up in your business for longer.

Investors

Very few investors will consider start-ups unless they have a very high growth capacity. But many are happy to lend their money – and sometimes even their expertise and contact lists – to small businesses looking to expand. Most investors will also only agree to fund a business if its form has limited liability – such as limited companies and limited liability partnerships. In exchange for a stake in your business, investors will give you money. Generally large sums are involved, over £10,000 most of the times. It is unlikely you would need that much for simply marketing a blog further.. But you might need this much if you decide to start several new blogs, employ people to help with content creation or management, or are hoping to start offering blogging services to others.

The advantage of finding investors is that they will only take their money back as and when the business makes enough profits to pay them back. Generally, this is paid through the dividends a limited company offers their share holders at the end of each tax year. There is no repayment to be made each month, and so no short term strain on your cashflow. However, you will need to keep in mind that your investors will generally want out fairly quickly, and with more money in their pockets than what they initially invested. As such, your business generally needs to have a high growth potential to be considered by most investors.

Venture capitalists will fund businesses and projects requiring large amounts of money – from £250,000 upwards – and showing very high growth potential. These are generally groups of people investing their money through a third party organisation. You will deal with this organisation, but not with the investors directly. They generally look for people who know what they are doing in business and in their industry. Some are willing to lend to start up businesses, but will be want a low-risk/high-return investment.

Business angels may be a better option for many start-ups. They provide funds to business with lower investment needs, some as low as £5,000. Many angels are also happy to be actively involved in the businesses they invest in. Some will even insist on it. They can become your very own business mentors, and can also provide you with the business contacts you need to break in your industry, or your chosen niche.

Approaching Potential Investors

When you think you are ready to go looking for more funds, it is time to make first contact. If you are looking to get more funds from your bank, then you need to get in touch with your bank manager. If you are trying to approach external investors, research where you can find them. In the UK, the Business Link website maintains a database of grants, venture capitalist organisations and business angels networks for you to approach. Alternatively, you can just do a quick search for them on the Internet.

The Potential Investors

If you cannot find any of these investors in your area, then you need to get creative. Who would maybe be interested in a partnership with you as you develop your own business? It could be that several other small businesses would be happy to invest in your own for various reasons. Maybe they want access to your services at a huge discount. Maybe they just want to expand their own business in this direction. Whatever their reasons, you might be able to strike a deal with them.

You should be prepared to present your ideas and your plans to the people you meet. Of course, your bank manager and formal investors will have a very precise idea of what they want from you in terms of business and/or marketing plan. You should try to match their expectation as closely as possible. It will both impress them and allow them to make their decision quicker.

You should also prepare what is called an elevator pitch. This is a two or three-minute speech that presents the bare bones of what you do, how much you need to expand, and how you would use the money. This could be very useful to approach less formal investors. More often than not, you will only get one shot at it. You basically need to convince them that your proposition is worth a look in more details. Always mention the fact that you have full business and marketing plans ready to be shown to potential investors. You should also remember that you're not trying to convince then to invest on the spot, just to consider the proposal before giving an answer.

5 – The Keys to Success

You now have most of the knowledge you need to make your blogging business a success. Many people also want to know all the secrets behind creating a successful business. Few strategies for success are secret. And the most common ingredients are determination and organisation. But there are a few things that you should keep in mind when planning for your business.

Blogging is more than managing blogs

It is important to keep in mind that a successful blogging business will do a lot more than creating good content and publishing it online. Non blogging operations such as bookkeeping and accounting, invoicing, HR – if you employ anyone – and marketing need to be dealt with in order to keep your business running smoothly. This is on top of researching audiences and niches, sourcing content, and marketing a particular blog. Using either Customer Relation Management (CRM) or Enterprise Resource Planning (ERP) systems, you can bring most of these operations into one place. This can help you reduce both starting and running costs, and reduce the amount of time used performing these tasks.

You should also keep in mind that people have become lazy on the Internet. They will only look through the first page of search results – maybe the second – and that's it. You will need

Blog

to push your content to them, while not selling it to them. It is a difficult balancing act. The best way to achieve this is to create a strong presence for your blog(s) and business on social networks. Using the likes of Twitter and Facebook, you can strike conversations with your readers without actually selling anything to them. Although it may seem like it, it is not a waste of time as it allows people to get to know you. Starting by laying a solid foundation of trust in your expertise, you will find that your readers will click through to your site more often when you do present them with links back to your blog.

There are many different tools that can help you manage various social networks from either one location on your computer, or straight from within your blog. TweetDeck, HootSuite, and MarketMeSuite are all very good software you can download to your computer and use to manage your presence on various social networks. If you would prefer to manage this from your blog, there are many extensions available for the major CMS and blogging platforms.

Tracking

In the business of blogging, everything comes down to tracking your results. Because the Internet is so fast-paced, you need to know which of your marketing strategy is still working, and which has already become obsolete. You need to know which site is still bringing in money through advertising, which keywords are losing grounds in terms of searches, which products are selling, which sites have the more visitors, how responsive your email lists are... The problem with this is that none of this data will be readily available to you if you do not make the effort of putting the relevant systems in place.

Google likes to make things easy for webmasters, because their ultimate goal is to make the Internet fast and easy to use for users. Google Analytics program can help you to track your visitors on your site. The Google AdWords keyword tool will show which keywords are often searched for through Google search. Feedburner will allow you to create, distribute, track, and monetize RSS feeds for your sites. If you are using the Google AdSense program to serve ads onto your sites, you can set it up so you know exactly which sites earn how much.

Another tool worth investing in is an email list manager. MailChimp, GetResponse, and Aweber are the best in the industry. They will allow you to take control of your lists and manage them effectively. They offer a good set of features, such as auto-responders, lists and customers management, tracking and design tools, integration with social media, and more.

Post Scheduling

We have already mentioned how important it is to decide early on how often you will be updating your blog(s) and stick to this. Of course, it is often easier said than done. It is however important to keep to your schedule as your regular readers may feel let down if that are expecting a post from you that never comes. And so developing a good blogging schedule for your site is necessary.

Of course, it will all start with ideas. You should keep up to date with the developments in your niche(s). Follow the news, speak with people interested to find out what they want to learn more about, talk to experts to learn more about the niche yourself. This will give you a near constant stream of content to be written. Keep a list of all the ideas you get, so you never run out of possible content for your site.

Define a schedule for your blog. How often will you blog, and when? If you are blogging everyday, at what time will you publish your post(s)? If you decide to only blog a couple of times a week, which days will you choose? These can be important for your blog and will depend on your audience. Once you know this, you can work out your researching, writing, and editing schedules. Of course, if you are sourcing content to re-distribute or having someone else create the content for you, you will only need to check for the quality of the content you receive. It could save you a lot of time, if not necessarily money.

Most CMS and blogging platforms have the ability to schedule posts. You can write six posts in one day, and then have them published over the course of the next three weeks – two posts a week. If this ability is not part of the core system, it usually can be added through modules. Some platforms can also be extended to show your schedule in a more visual way than the common list of post published and to be published.

140

Market, Market, and Market Some More

Even if you have the greatest content around, it will not bring visitors to your site. SEO will only go so far, and it's unlikely you will see a huge number of visitors flooding your site everyday while relying only on search engines. You need to work at marketing your blog every day. We have given you all the marketing tools you might need, and it's up to you to see which ones work best for your blog.

Social media have become one of the best ways to market your blog. People have become very lazy on the Internet and they do not search for content as they use to. Social networks allow you to both get in touch with people who share your interests, and for them to follow what you are up to on your blog. Social bookmarking has become a very popular way to search for content. Because the content is sorted and rated by real users, the social bookmarks cannot be abused in the same way as the search engines – which can still fall prey to irrelevant keywords and advertising.

Another important strategy to great blog marketing is link building. Link building can work two ways for your blog. Incoming links to your blog will improve your SEO efforts, and in turn boost your ranking in search engines. If this is your primary objective, you should make sure that all your incoming links are set to 'do-follow'. Another objective could simply be to direct people to your people to blog – as opposed to the search engines' spiders. In this case, it doesn't matter if the incoming links are set to no-follow or do-follow. People will click them and be directed to your site anyway.

6 – Glossary

Above the fold – This is a newspaper term. Imagine your newspaper folded in half, as it is on a newspapers stand. Everything that can be seen without unfolding the paper is 'above the fold'. The same applies to your blog. Everything that can be seen without scrolling down is 'above the fold'.

Archive – This is the place on your blog where your older posts will be stored. They will still be available to your readers looking for something in particular, or just for what you have written before.

Blogosphere – This terms refers to all the blogs that can be found on the Internet.

Blogroll – This is a collection of links to other blogs. These blogs are usually relevant to one common subject.

Category – One way to organize content on your site. All posts that relate to a particular subject within your niche can be put under a category to allow readers to find what they are looking for more quickly.

CMS – Stands for Content Management System. This is the general term given to software designed to make it easier for non-technical people to create and manage their own websites. Most CMS can be used to create blogs.

6 – Glossary

Comment – A reply to the content posted. This is how bloggers can get feedback, and one way to engage your readers in conversations.

CPC – Stands for Cost Per Click. A form of online advertising, where you get paid when people click on the ad you are displaying on your site.

CPM – Literally Cost Per Thousand, it stand for Cost Per Impression. Another form of online advertising, where you are paid by the number of times the ads appear on your site. The price is usually set per thousand views.

CSS – Stands for Cascading Style Sheet. This code is what designers now use to create the design of websites, along with HTML.

Dashboard – This is the place on your blog from which you can manage everything that happens on it: posting content, changing design, adding new features and widgets...

Flame – This is a generally nasty and personal comment. It has little to do with the actual content published on the blog.

Footer – The area at the bottom of your blog. It generally carries copyright, design and developmental information about the site, such as whom legally claims the content as their own, who designed the site, and which CMS or blogging platform is used as its basis.

Header – The area at the top of your blog. It generally carries your blog name and/or logo, and some navigational items. Some people put ads there to take advantage of the 'above the fold' position.

Keyword – A keyword can be a single word or a phrase (usually called a long tail keyword). They will be used within content, HTML tags, or online ads to help search engines give relevant content to their users.

Main content – The area of your site where your content will displayed. On your homepage, this will be a collection of links to your posts, organised by date and/or subject. On your post pages, it may display your actual content, ads, and/or additional navigational items – such as breadcrumbs or *return to top* link.

Navigational item – Named links that will allow your readers to navigate around your site more easily. This can include your menus, sitemaps, categories, breadcrumbs, archive, and more.

Niche – A subject that a blog or website will concentrate on. This can be very narrow such as how to lose weight by dieting, or a broader subject like how to live a healthy life.

Permalink – The structure that the links within your site will take. Each of your post will be given a specific link, so it is still easily available once it is put into your archive.

Ping – A way to send notification of your blog's updates. This will usually automatically be sent by your software to search engines and blog aggregators. These will them show your content in their search results when relevant.

RSS – Stands for Really Simple Syndication. Most CMS and blogging platforms will automatically generate a RSS feed, an XML file that can be picked up and distributed by content aggregators. An easy way to distribute your content to some who might not know about you otherwise.

Search engine – Online directories maintaining databases of almost every piece of content available of the Internet. Users use keywords to search for content, and search engines will display results accordingly.

SEO – Stands for Search Engine Optimization. A series of tools that will help to boost the amount of traffic your site receives from search engines.

Sidebar – The area to the side of your main content. Sidebars can be found on one or both side of the main content. They will usually carry navigational items – such as menus, links to the archive and categories, tag cloud – ads, links to social networks profiles, and ways to subscribe to the blog – such as email or RSS.

Social media – These will include social networks, such as Facebook, Twitter, and LinkedIn, as well as social bookmarking sites, like Reddit, StumbleUpon, Digg and Del.icio.us. They allow users to communicate, find and review content of interest, and exchange tips and ideas, across the world and on a daily basis if they so wish.

6 – Glossary

Tag – A way to organize the content on your site. Not to be confused with HTML tags. Content tags allow readers to find all the posts relevant to the tag in one go. Tags were first used by social bookmarking sites to organize their own content.

Theme – This is a website template. They are used to change what a blog looks like. They will usually be written in a mix of CSS and HTML. If the theme was designed around a particular CMS or blogging platform, they will also be using the code language of that software (often PHP).

Trackback – A communication tool between sites. Generally automatic, your site will receive notices when other blogs link to your content, and vice versa.

URL – Stands for Uniform/Universal Resource Locator. This is basically the address of your domain name, and every posts and pages on your site. It will generally look like this: http://www.yourdomain.com/file-path-to/your-content

Widget – Small apps usually found in the sidebar(s) and footer areas of a blog. They can serve various purposes, from managing advertising, to integrating your social profiles on your blog, and much more.

7 – Resources

Here you will find as many resources as we could fit at the end of this book. It might be useful to have a look at these as you prepare to launch you new business venture.

Useful Books

On Blogging as a Business
ProBlogger: Secrets for Blogging Your Way to a Six-Figure Income by Darren Rowse and Chris Garrett

Start Your Own Blogging Business, 2nd Edition by Jason R. R. Rich

On Business
How They Started: How 30 good ideas became great businesses by David Lester

The Entrepreneur's Book of Checklists: 1000 Tips to Help You Start and Grow Your Business by Robert Ashton

How to Start Your Own Business for Entrepreneurs by Robert Ashton

Useful Books

Start Your Business: Week by Week by Steve Parks

On Writing
100 Ways to Find Ideas for Your Blog Posts by Steven Aitchison

Sticky Readers: How To Attract a Loyal Blog Audience By Writing More Better by Margaret Andrews

Write First, Clean Later: Blogs, Articles, & Writing Advice by L.J. Sellers

1,001 Writing Prompts to Ignite Your Creative Spark: For Fiction and Non-Fiction Writers Who Want to Break Free From Writer's Block and Hone Their Writing Skills by Heather R. Wallace

Useful Websites

Blogging-related
Alexa – This site measures the traffic on other websites. This can be extremely useful to know when planning your SEO efforts. They are various Internet browser's extensions you can use to save you time and get this data while you are reviewing the sites you'd like to work with.
http://www.alexa.com

Amazon Associates – A very useful affiliate programme. It has the advantage of being run by a very famous company, and giving you access to an incredible range of products to promote. The combination makes it difficult to resist. You can sign up on the international site, or your localized version. Or both.
https://www.affiliate-program.amazon.com

Clickbank – A well-known affiliate program in the Internet marketing circles. It is centred around digital products. Conversion rates can be quite good, especially since merchants will usually provide you with a good range of selling tools.
http:/www.clickbank.com

CopyBlogger – Another blog full of great content, this time by the developer of the Genesis Framework for WordPress. Full of great advice about Internet marketing, copywriting, and blogging in general. If you want to learn more about these subjects, have a look through their

tutorials section, and sign up for their free Internet Marketing course.
http://www.copyblogger.com

DailyBlogTips – Yet another good blog about blogging. They have good advice on many of
the facets of blogging: strategy, design, content, SEO, monetizing... If you are going to use
WordPress as your blogging platform, you may want to sign up for their newsletter as they
will give you a small collection of themes for free.
http://www.dailyblogtips.com

Delicious – A bookmarking site. You can both get your site bookmarked, and provide
additional information to your own readers by bookmarking other website and blogs of
interest.
http://delicious.com

Digg – Social bookmarking site that allow their users to vote for their favourite sites by
'digging' them.
http://www.digg.com

Facebook – Popular social network. Need not say more really.
http://www.facebook.com

Google – The Internet giant, providing too many services to list them all. As a blogger, you
might want to sign up with at least their Analytics, Webmaster Tools, AdSense, Alerts, and
Apps programmes. You may want to submit your blog and posts to both their main search
engine and their blog search engine. They also now own Feedburner and YouTube, so it's
difficult to escape them.
http://www.google.com

ProBlogger – One of the most respected blog about blogging, and making a profit from it.
Full of tips and ideas to improve your efforts, both in terms of content development and
marketing. The blog is written by Darren Rowse, a long time, professional blogger and author
of ProBlogger: Secrets for Blogging Your Way to a Six-Figure Income and 31 Days to Build a
Better Blog.
http://www.problogger.net

Reddit – Social bookmarking site that work in the same way as Digg, in that users will vote
for their favourite sites and content.
http://www.reddit.com

StumbleUpon – Another social bookmarking site, where user will rate your content.
StumbleUpon them makes this review available to other users, and uses it to rank your site.
http://www.stumbleupon.com

Useful Websites

Technorati – This site is extremely useful for research purposes. You can find blogs related to your content, and data on the blogging industry. They publish the State of the Blogosphere reports, very useful to see what is going on in the world of blogging. They are a blog search engine. You can submit your blog to be added to their database. Their users may then find your content if it is relevant to their search.
http://www.technorati.com

Twitter – A social network in the form of a micro-blogging platform.
http://www.twitter.com

Yahoo! - Another major company on the Internet. They own a search engine, and have create their Buzz programme to act as a social bookmarking site, and Publisher Network programme to serve advertising in a way similar to that of the Google AdSense programme.
http://www.yahoo.com

Business-related

Business Link – The website and the network of local offices associated with it makes this the ultimate resources for anyone looking to start or expand a business in the UK. Through them you can find training, funding, and networking opportunities in your region.
http://www.businesslink.org.uk

Chamber of Commerce – Your local branch may be offering training to both members and non-members. They will also be a wealth of contacts, so it can be a very good move to approach them even if you can't afford the membership fee yet.
http://www.britishchambers.org.uk

MarketResearch.com – A very useful site if you are looking for in depth reports about a particular industry. The costs are quite prohibitive, but you may be able to gather the information you need from the summaries published to promote the actual reports.
http://www.marketresearch.com

Open University – Although they have no course to help you develop your blogging skills, the Open University offers a range of certificate that will teach you the basics of business management. If you lack business training or management experience, one of this certificate might be a good idea.
http://www.open.ac.uk

Prince's Trust – A good place to go to for free business training if you are between the age of 18 and 30 years. They will give you the basics and will help you to come up with a business plan. At the end of your training, you even get the chance to win funding from their panel. The last few years, their funding has run pretty dry, and so it is now very difficult to get a loan from them. Still the standing in front of the panel explaining your business plan is a good

exercise to go through.
http://www.princes-trust.org.uk

Scavenger – A very useful site maintained by CobWebInfo, where you can buy reports to help you research your business idea. Although they do not have anything about blogging at the time of writing, it may be useful to research your niche subject.
http://www.scavenger.net

UK Business Forums – A good place to make contacts around the country and get help from other entrepreneurs.
http://www.ukbusinessforums.co.uk

Warrior Forum – Although aimed at Internet marketers, you can still find very useful contacts, advice, and ideas on these forums.
http://www.warriorforum.com

Index

www.ingramcontent.com/pod-product-compliance
Lightning Source LLC
Chambersburg PA
CBHW081450170526
45166CB00008B/2379